rise up

rise up

The #Merky Story So Far

Stormzy

With contributions from Team #Merky
Images by Kaylum Dennis
Edited and Co-written by Jude Yawson

1 3 5 7 9 10 8 6 4 2

#Merky Books
20 Vauxhall Bridge Road
London SW1V 2SA

#Merky Books is part of the Penguin Random House
group of companies whose addresses can be found at
global.penguinrandomhouse.com.

Penguin
Random House
UK

First published by #Merky Books in 2018
This paperback edition published by #Merky Books in 2019

www.penguin.co.uk

A CIP catalogue record for this book is available
from the British Library.

ISBN 9781529118520

Text and plate sections designed by Lindsay Nash

Printed and bound in Great Britain by Clays Ltd, Elcograf S.p.A.

Penguin Random House is committed to a sustainable future
for our business, our readers and our planet. This book
is made from Forest Stewardship Council® certified paper.

MIX
Paper from
responsible sources
FSC® C018179

To my team, my family. Thank you for holding me down and protecting me. For helping me to manifest and make sense of all these crazy ideas that run through my head. I wake up every single day knowing that I can achieve absolutely anything by sending one text in a group chat. How flipping powerful is that? I love and appreciate every single one of you.

And I guess this book is for the dreamers and the doubtful alike. Ask yourself 'What am I afraid of?' and then laugh at your answer. Laugh at it, point at it, ridicule it and then go and get your f****** dream. It's yours. And I swear to God nothing can stop you.

And finally, to this mighty God I serve, thank you for your favour and your grace. You have never let me down.

Akua

It's really weird. You never realise that you're on a journey until you look back on it. You just get up every day and you work, you do whatever you've got to do that day. It's only when you stop and think that it starts to make sense.

contents

list of contributors   xi
introduction   1

part 1:   **preparation**
          introduction   11
          1   15
          2   28
          3   53

part 2:   **work**
          introduction   73
          4   77
          5   95
          6   104

part 3:   **execution**
          introduction   119
          7   123
          8   134
          9   150

part 4:   **ambition**
          introduction   173
          10   177
          11   189
          12   207

timeline   221

discography   227

list of illustrations   230

list of contributors

Akua Agyemfra
Cultural strategist and Team #Merky brand manager, and
#Merky Group Director. Dabble in music and I've got an actual
MSc in Football. North London.

Alec Boateng/Twin B
Co-Head of A&R Atlantic Records UK, Broadcaster/DJ 1Xtra,
Stormzy's broseph.

Rachel Campbell
Stormzy's publicist. From Bedford, Bedfordshire. Moved to
south London aged twenty-one. Part of the #Merky team since
February 2015.

Austin Daboh
Head of Editorial, Spotify UK. South London.

Kaylum Dennis
Music Video Director, with responsibility for Tour and Visual
Content for Stormzy. From Brixton Hill, south London.

Flipz
#Merky Records President. Croydon, south London.

Manon Grandjean
Recording engineer and mixer from the South of France.

Ayesha Lorde Dunn

Team #Merky Manager. #Merky Management and Team #Merky EA. North London.

Tobe Onwuka

Stormzy's manager and Co-Founder of #Merky. South London.

Fraser T. Smith

Music producer and songwriter. West London.

Stormzy

Musician and Co-Founder of #Merky. Norbury/Thornton Heath, south London.

DJ TiiNY

Stormzy's DJ. South London.

Trevor A. Williams

Tour Manager and Head of Touring for Stormzy Live. #Merky Team Player. North London.

Jude Yawson

Philosophy graduate. Writer of essays, articles, poetry, film reviews, and in the future – novels, films, TV shows and documentaries. Aiming to be the greatest black British writer ever. Crystal Palace, south-east London.

rise up

introduction

Jude

There's a video on YouTube I can watch again and again. It's
the moment Stormzy wins Album of the Year at the Brit Awards
in February 2018. There's no build-up in the clip; Nile Rodgers
just embraces the mic and shouts, 'Stormzzzzyyyyyyy!' You get
the sense that he's happy with the result. The camera then
pans to Stormzy's table, showing a mob of friends celebrating.
There's no sign of the man himself. You can see Flipz, #Merky
President and probably the longest-serving member of the
team, jumping up and down like he's scored a worldie. You can
see Michael Dapaah screaming. You can see Tobe, his manager
and good friend from Thornton Heath, slapping the back of
someone in the centre of the picture. And then that someone
begins to move: it's a man with his head in his hands.

Stormzy is wearing a black T-shirt and tracksuit
trousers – possibly the same ones he'll wear during his
performance later that night. He gets up and begins to walk
away from the table, pushed on by his team, but runs straight
into Fraser T. Smith, the producer he worked with on the
album for over ten months. They give each other a hug. Maybe
words are said, but you can't really tell. He's in a bit of a daze.
And suddenly you start to notice the song 'Blinded by Your
Grace, Pt. 2' playing as he walks towards the stage and up
the steps. It's the moment in the song when the chorus fades

and the uplifting bridge breaks through. It's almost perfectly timed: 'Said a prayer this morning, I prayed I would find the way . . .' sounds out amid the clapping as Stormzy walks forward, hands clasped together, eyes looking ahead.

It's not the first time someone's won Album of the Year at the Brits, and it won't be the last. For some people it's not a particularly special moment at all. For others it really is. What does it mean? Why does it matter to me? Why does it matter at all? That's really what this book is about.

I started to write in 2012 with the aim of one day making a living from it. Looking back, I was embarking on a journey with no firm foundations or solid examples for my unrealistic ambitions. There were, back then, no contemporary black British writers I wanted to emulate. No figure with a catalogue of work I wanted to mimic. But as much as I was looking for someone who represented me, the lack of anyone was in some ways an incentive to keep trying.

Six years later and I'm writing these words. In a sense, I am not really supposed to be. Like the subject of this book, I am from a troubled part of south-east London. At school, I was never touted for greatness, and was expelled when I was thirteen. I joined a pupil referral unit, where I became friends with gang members, victims of abuse and an array of children who'd been cast out of mainstream education. Drama and danger were never strangers. I spent a lot of time back then writing, without knowing why I was doing it, or for whom. I thought I had potential, but potential can be an empty word with no parameters. A teacher once told me that if I was ever stabbed I should keep the knife inside my body, rather than remove it, to prevent myself from dying. I was never violent, but I remember how simply I absorbed that lesson – a young person with no expectations of any type of meaningful future, anticipating a meaningless death. I got my GCSEs, however, and started my A levels, though I still had no real idea of where I was going.

Getting kicked out of school had made me look at life differently. There is a universal African diaspora truth that I eventually realised: as a black person you have to work twice as hard. I'd made life even harder for myself by hitting rock bottom at a young age. I think back on growing up and I feel troubled by the mentality we all had, the lack of hope. We settled for less and filled the void of 'what if' with other ideas. Any deviation from that mindset prompted strange responses. The stigma would persist until someone actually did something. But what could we do?

Being born and existing as a Ghanaian in a Eurocentric society meant being on the outside. At school I was never taught about black British history, but I started to teach myself, gaining an understanding of those who worked to fight against discrimination and racist systems. I had a sense that it could be a first step in challenging my worldview, and that of my peers – a way to make sense of the present by acknowledging the past.

My knowledge of contemporary black Britishness came through television and music. *The Lenny Henry Show*. Groups like Cleopatra, Big Brovaz, Mis-Teeq and So Solid Crew. Artists like Craig David, Ms. Dynamite and Estelle. They presented scenes of unfiltered black Britishness. But they still seemed like something 'other' – a few steps removed from my life, rare exceptions rather than the rule.

At the same time, however, there was an underground scene bubbling up. A scene that would spread from London across the UK, captivating a generation who related to its energy, its rawness and its message. This was grime: both a culture and an identity. It was something closer to home. I was a grime kid and I was privileged to witness its historic rise. I watched my brother record sets on cassette. We bought blank CDs and traded tracks with our friends. South London had immense grime MCs like the Roadside G's, South Soldiers, N-Double-A. But grime's homeland was at a distance, in Bow, E3. We watched Bow local Dizzee Rascal record his 'Jus' a Rascal' video on a boat while David Blaine sat in a box suspended above the Thames. And by the time I was starting to dream about writing for a living, Dizzee was performing at the opening ceremony of the London Olympics. All of a sudden, the whole world was watching.

I first noticed Stormzy on Facebook, via mutual friends' comments. Then he won the Unsigned Stars competition. I started doing a bit of digging, and found a few of his freestyle videos on YouTube. They were captivating. There was a hunger and an energy about him that was completely new. Here was a raw yet swaggering MC, intelligent, uncompromising and lyrically gifted. It was no wonder people were saying, 'He's going to blow.' What's more, he was one of us. From the ends, Thornton Heath. Every success of his felt like a victory for all of us.

His rise has been meteoric. In a little over four years he

has progressed from unsigned hopeful to one of the most influential British cultural figures of today – an MC whose first album went straight to number one and broke a number of records in the process. But he has never been just an MC. Stormzy's artistry is elusive, but it could be put down to an unmatched level of honesty and foresight, aided by faith in God.

He's also aided by a team like no other: Tobe, Akua, Ayesha, Rachel, Trevor, TiiNY, Kaylum and Flipz. Fraser, Manon, Alec (aka Twin B) and Austin have also provided invaluable support at various stages. There are other figures who I did not get the opportunity to meet but whose names are mentioned in the text: most importantly Craig and Fran, Stormzy's booking agents, and Kieran, Stormzy's lawyer, who I know have all done a huge amount, and have repeatedly gone above and beyond to get the team to where they are today. I liken them to the Avengers. Each has their own superpower but all have a strikingly close idea of what to do and say. Stormzy describes it as a #Merky DNA, which is a better way of putting it. His team are the dynamic force behind him, who help bring his ideas to life as well as helping each other realise their own goals.

Growing up, few if any of us could have envisaged the entirety of what Stormzy and the team have achieved on their own terms: the success, the respect, the bridging of cultures, the giving back, the ambition. The #Merky journey is about never settling for less. #Merky might just seem like a selling point, but I think it's more than that. It is a family. It is a level of work, a standard to uphold, and a way of thinking.

That night at the Brits, Stormzy began his acceptance speech by thanking God. 'I know it seems like such a strange thing,' he says, 'but if you know God you know that this is all Him.' Then he thanks Fraser and Manon, then his team, then his family. Making the album was the hardest thing he's done, he says, and he put everything into it. I wanted to know what that meant.

There were a few things I knew before I started this book. I knew who the team were, and I knew they had done a lot themselves, maybe more than any other team without the support of a major label has done before. I knew that they gave back – I myself being one of the benefactors of their success. I wrote something about Stormzy in 2014, posted it online, and he made contact directly to thank me. I'm not the only one he's reached out to in this way. I had heard stories about their work ethic, and about their influence. And I had a lot of questions for them and for Stormzy: how did the team come together? What were your initial aims? What did you want to achieve, and why? How does it feel to be one of very few black men in our country at the height of stardom? Mentally, how does one cope with the pressure and expectations that comes with success? How did you write the album? What were your influences? What does performing live feel like? Who are your heroes? I got most of the answers, and a lot more.

There are a couple of important things to mention before we begin. Our aim with *Rise Up* was to present the story of team #Merky as faithfully as we could. I conducted interviews with thirteen members of the core and extended team over a two-month period – interviews which were then transcribed and organised to try and describe the last four years in some recognisable sequence. This is my version of their story however, and so it can never be complete. I am aware that there are some gaps in the narrative, and some important people whose voices are not included here. Each contributor is credited at the start of their sections, and there is a full list as well as short biographies of all those included at the beginning of the book. As the book is essentially a sequence of transcriptions, you will find that it doesn't read the same way it would if it had been rewritten. I have tried to stick as closely as possible to what was said, rather than rework or embellish anyone's words. Fidelity seemed more important than flow. I've also written short introductions to each of the book's four parts to articulate the key moments covered in some way.

After Stormzy's initial message of appreciation in 2014, we stayed in touch. He commented on my writing, and I did what I could to support his career. He asked me to help him create this book. He could easily have secured an established writer with decades of experience, but he asked me, someone who has never worked on a book before. I hope that it does him and the team justice. I know this is going to sound corny, but I hope, above all else, that the story it tells offers you what it offered to me: inspiration.

preparation

You know what it is, yeah? It's not even the fact that I'm, that I'm underrated or, or the fact that I'm, I'm being slept on. It's the, it's the fact that people don't think I'm a threat, do you understand? People don't think that I'm, that I'm the one to be, to be looked out for, one to be watched. And that's when it becomes a problem, that's when I have to rise up and become a problem, do you understand?

'The Intro', 168: The Mixtape

introduction

Jude

Without trying to sound too overblown, it's very easy to look back on Stormzy's early career and think that there was something preordained about his rise. In one of my last interviews with him, we talked a lot about God, and about having belief in Him to help you realise your goals, as well as having belief in yourself. Considering the world that Stormzy came from, it would have been easy to turn to other means to get ahead, like the friends who 'lost so much of their childhood because they wanted more', as Tobe puts it. But Stormzy had a path. Part 1 is about that path, and about the paths of the other members of the team. The paths that led them into music, and the paths that brought them together.

There were several characteristics that all of the team members shared even before they came together: ambition, initiative, a strong work ethic, a striving for excellence and, perhaps most importantly, foresight. The ability to not only dream, but to see how their dreams could be realised. Characteristics, as I've said, that Stormzy describes as the #Merky DNA, which connect the team more as a family than as a business outfit.

Stormzy was a young up-and-coming MC with endless bars, and he quickly reached a point where he had to take a leap to do what he loved. Tobe was working hard to support his family, but he was always there for his friend. Kaylum was a young videographer with a name for himself but no plan B. TiiNY was beginning to see where his DJing could lead. Akua knew who she wanted to work for and why. And Trevor was tired of seeing his artists being let down at the last minute, and thought he could do something to change that.

South London in the early 2000s was an interesting place, musically. Growing up, my family listened to a lot of Motown or graceful Ghanaian highlife on vinyl, interspersed with the music of Eddy Grant, Maxi Priest, George Michael and David Bowie – these were my first tastes of a British sound. In other homes, R&B and the new home-grown rhythms of jungle and garage were giving way to something else. This was grime: a music that was soon bellowing out in homes across the country. In this part we will first hear from Alec and Austin: two people who witnessed and helped to realise the rise of grime, as DJ/A&R and programmer respectively. They were the champions of the black British sound: promoting music, putting out and playing records, organising events, and creating the connections that would help younger artists gain a foothold on the ladder. It is these two, as much as any others, who helped to shape the musical tastes of a generation, and who made a significant contribution to the musical scene that Stormzy became obsessed with. Fraser T. Smith, meanwhile, was helping to take one of black Britain's biggest stars to new heights, and was also laying the foundations for an extraordinary career as a producer.

This part tells all of these stories, and more. That's why we've decided to call it Preparation. You can establish a simple narrative for #Merky's formation and early success without too much trouble, but what's missing is the preparation: the work and thought that went into finding a way forward and being a part of something, and the trust and confidence that was required to follow that path.

1.

Stormzy

Where I grew up and how I grew up really affected how I saw the world. This may be a bit of a generalisation, but I think for most people, having particular dreams, and seeing a way to realise them is a normal thing. It might be something as simple as a dream job, for example, and recognising the steps that need to be taken to get that job. We didn't have that. Where I'm from that doesn't really happen. People might have the skills they need to get their dream job, but they can't see a way to get there.

That's why I've always said that my career is God. My whole career is of faith. It's beyond me being an anomaly or tapping into a particular skill set. It's His grace and favour. We're from a place where success doesn't happen. I didn't have access to any special knowledge, and I wasn't given anything to help me on my way. I had the same things that everyone else in my area had. All I had was an unbreakable level of confidence. It was beyond confidence, actually. Beyond perseverance, or

beyond arrogance. It was certainty – a certainty in my future.
I didn't just dream of being successful – I *knew* I was going to
be successful. It wasn't a joke.

It comes from my mum, because my mum was always very
supportive. And God. That level of confidence is a blessing.
Not everyone has that kind of belief in themselves. It was
normal at the time, but looking back, it was strange. That's
some sort of divine favour. I was around thirty or forty young
brothers who had no hope – who were hopeless. Not hopeless
as people, but without hope for their future, because of where
we were coming from. I was like: Nah. Man's got all the hope.

It didn't come from anywhere apart from a sense that I
could do it.

Alec (Twin)

I grew up in east London – Bethnal Green, Bow and Plaistow.
My parents used to listen to a lot of R&B and soul music:
Lionel Ritchie, the Commodores, that kind of thing. And also
a lot of Ghanaian music, highlife, artists like Daddy Lumba
and others.

My first real interest in music was CDs, and being obsessed
with the radio! I just used to collect CDs of whatever was
popular at the time, and play them constantly. Nineties R&B
and hip hop, primarily, but a lot of other stuff as well. And a
lot of radio.

In east London during my teens there was plenty going
on in the music scene. I had a few friends at school who
were into music, but I also knew people in the years above

from my area who were DJing, MCing, going on pirate radio and things like that. Even my older brother started MCing. It was easy to get into. Just get the records. All you needed was the ten key records and you're a DJ. If you had enough bars you could become an MC. There were loads of people making music, too. My good friend DJ Wonder was making music, Wiley was making music, Dizzee Rascal was making music. You could even use a PlayStation to make beats. There were quite a few people who made some seminal grime tracks on a PlayStation.

Austin

My early relationship with music was really shaped by my parents and my brothers and sisters. I'm the youngest child of six, from a big Nigerian family, and I had to listen to what they listened to, whether I liked it or not. I'm an eighties baby, and I began to be aware of music when I was five or six years old. It was really the sound of black British households at that moment. It was Soul II Soul, it was Michael Jackson, it was Madonna, it was whatever was hot and popular.

I only started to develop my own taste in music in the mid-nineties, when jungle was big. My sister had a boyfriend who was a typical jungle fan, he had a BMW convertible M3, and he used to take me and my sister driving around London blaring out jungle. That was the first moment I thought: What is this sound? It isn't pop, it isn't hip hop, what is it? From that point on I've followed the twists and turns of the black British music experience: from jungle to garage in the late nineties, phase one of grime in the early noughties, and hip hop threaded throughout that. But I used to listen to all sorts, really.

Before jungle you had a lot of British acts adopting an American persona. To be fair, you had people like London Posse, respect to them, but it was only really with jungle that you began to see a UK musical form come through. I mean, jungle was closer to home, even though it wasn't necessarily British, as so much of the chatting was in patois – but we heard that accent in our friends' houses. People often forget about jungle in terms of the evolution of MC-led music. When jungle came, it was on your doorstep. The people who were making it looked like you. American rappers had the oversized clothes and the big dooky gold chain, but the jungle MCs had the little sovereign, or the gold tooth, which I could get from H. Samuel or Trotters, do you know what I mean?

Alec (Twin)

You could tell that something was happening, and that there was a scene developing, and a culture forming around that scene. It didn't feel like it came from any particular place. It didn't feel like an evolution at the time. It felt completely new. It was pirate radio, and crews, and DJ sets, and club nights, and it was all people we knew, friends of friends. My older brother was at Blessed John Roche School, and was good friends with Major Ace. And they were all friends with Wiley, Target, Danny Weed and all of them. My twin was at college with Janaya, Wiley's sister. A lot of my friends were involved.

My friend Terry had a birthday party in Year 10, and as I had loads of CDs and all the latest R&B and hip hop imports, I ended up DJing. It was a house party, and I was just putting CDs in and out of the CD player. A year before that I saw my primary school friend Marvin, DJ Carnage, playing at another party, and something clicked. I knew I had a passion for playing music. It was hearing something I loved, and then wanting everyone else to love it.

I started collecting vinyl. My close friend Crisis had some decks. He got bought some 1210s, which were really expensive. So his house became the centre of the universe. We used to spend loads of time DJing there, and lots of different people used to turn up. The Ruff Sqwad boys, for example. At that time, if you were a DJ you were a hub. Anyone with decks and a mic in their house always had everyone there. That was how it worked. It was easy enough to get into, but there was a bit of a barrier to entry. Records were expensive. Decks were really expensive.

To play on pirate radio at that time, you had to pay subs. I think it was £60 or so, which when you're a teenager is a huge amount of money. So you could get into it easily enough, but you had to really want it to take it anywhere. That was a big filter for a lot of people. There was also an element of competition, especially if you were an MC. It was hard to get the mic, so you had to make sure you had your bars ready when you got it. You could easily spot who had talent and the magic. You could switch on pirate radio – like, say, *Deja Vu* on a Monday and Dizzee might pop up on a Ruff Sqwad crew set between four and six, or Kano with Nasty at eight! They would be the ones to get all the reloads. From early on, Dizzee was obviously the guy. I guess that was the start of my A&R career in some ways.

Austin

I was going to secondary school at a time in the nineties when garage culture was at its peak. Youth clubs were massive back then. Every single area in London had two or three youth clubs, and each one had decks and mics. Everyone in my school spat, we all had names, and our names were connected to our graffiti names, tagging and that. So we used to go to the youth clubs and spit. I realised very quickly that I was a really bad MC. My flow was weak, my delivery was bad, my voice was off.

But I was really good at analysing other people, and I was really good at setting the scene, if you know what I mean. And this was at the time when affordable hand-held cameras were popular. So I borrowed a camera from the school tech department and made music videos, basically, even though I didn't realise that was what I was doing.

At the same time, my mum got a job where they gave her a computer so that she could do some work at home. I was the only person in my estate who had a computer, so I became a hub for school friends or people from the area to come and get CDs burned and that kind of thing. I was the only person who could use Photoshop as well, so a lot of local artists used to come to me to make visuals, and I started working with them, as a product manager of sorts. One of the best local MCs, Smiler, was a friend of mine. And because he was my friend and I was the only person who had a computer and knew how to use it, I started working with him as his manager.

Alec (Twin)

Dizzee was the guy. He'd be grabbing mics at raves and everyone would go mad. Him and Wiley were battering pirate radio together. I remember listening to Dizzee with a friend from college before he was really known, and the friend just dismissed him. Then 'I Luv U' came out. From early on, it always felt like he was another one who might do more. We didn't know what more was, but knew that he was the guy that was going to push it forward.

That was when I started being interested in what was going on behind the scenes, in how the music was made.

There was also a bit of a mini economy within the scene at that time. I remember Wiley booked me for a rave, somewhere out of London, and he gave me £50 before I left. This was when my twin and I (who DJ together) were sixteen or seventeen. I remember thinking: Wow, there's money to be made here. I always scraped the money together. So through DJing I got to know quite a few new people, and started getting a bit better. But although this was the era of garage, or the very early days of grime, I was more into hip hop and R&B. I think if we'd been less into that we might have been a bit more involved in what was going on. I ended up having a few slots on pirate radio in any case. Wiley was doing four of five shows on different radio stations most days back then, and they'd also given him his own regular slot on Rinse FM, the *Wiley Kat Show*, on a Sunday night. He called me up and asked if my bro and I wanted to play for the first hour or so every week, starting things off with a hip hop set, so I said yes. He didn't actually turn up to his first two shows so, as it happened, I ended up playing for a lot longer than an hour each time. It was fun – we loved it.

That was the first time I met Lethal Bizzle, for example. One of DJ Wonder's MCs was a guy called Pepper. We were at Rinse and he had a lyric that mentioned More Fire Crew, which Lethal B was a part of, and so Lethal B turned up outside the station on his motorbike to check if it was a clash lyric or not.

It had felt quite unreal when major labels started paying attention, too. I mean, you had Dizzee and Wiley signing six-figure deals. No one really knew who XL, or most labels to be honest, were, but it didn't matter. These were people we knew getting 'signed'. People who were still around. Major Ace also used to talk a lot about how various labels were chasing him down, Sony and EMI and others, and despite what was going on I didn't really believe him. Once he called me up and said, 'I've got a freestyle for you,' and I went round and just sat in his house with his mum for two hours waiting for him to turn up . . . And he didn't. Anyway, I took everything he said with a pinch of salt. But then one day he was like, 'Yeah, so we're signed to Sony now.' And he was, for 'Champagne Dance'. Major Ace was a pioneer and a legend. A lot started with him.

Stormzy

I have a strange relationship with music. If I hear a piece of music I like, I can't let go. It's a mad, beautiful relationship. Growing up, I didn't listen to a lot of albums, but I did listen to a lot of songs. Little things. Firstly, gospel, at church. It's quite funny, because I got the keys to my new house the other day, and I went along with my mum and Flipz, and I asked her to say a prayer when we got there. She started singing, and I said, 'Wait a second, wait a second!' She sang the melody again, and it instantly connected. It was a song from church. It stuck with me. I still love it. I still remember being in church, and hearing the choir sing 'Bow Down and Worship Him', and there was one guy who used to change the notes for the last two words, so he was singing in harmony. Sweet melodies. And it always got me. The little things like that.

My sister used to listen to a lot of R&B, so I got into that, too. Then it was grime, Channel U. I missed the radio set days, I can't lie. My sister was into pirate radio, but I was too young. I went to a rave with my sister when I was in Year 6, a shubz, with people spitting on the mic. I was so tired that I fell asleep in the corner. She sent me home. I had to walk back up the hill on my own. Channel U was my era – Bomb Squad, Nasty Crew, all of them.

DJ TiiNY

When I was at school I was hyperactive. I was jarring. I just wouldn't give the teachers a rest. We had the best laughs. I got sent out of class all the time. I wouldn't even care. I wouldn't even care if they told my mum. So I got kicked out of school. I was sent to an educational centre in Mitcham, and missed the whole of Year 8. Suddenly I felt very lonely. I just thought: Fuck this. What am I going to do now? I remember talking to the teacher towards the end of the year, and just said, 'Miss, I'm smart, but I can be a bit silly. I really don't think I deserve to be here. If there are any schools that might want me, can you please let me know?' I had to flip the script.

I started at a new school, and knew a few people there, so it was OK. All the kids from around there used to meet up in Wimbledon after school, so I saw friends from my old school with friends from my new school, and just thought: You lot have done so much stuff without me. I just had to move on, switch it up.

Ayesha

I grew up just off Russell Square. The first time I told Mike, he was like, 'Where the hell is that?' I said, 'Tottenham Court Road. Oxford Street, you know.' He said, 'What, so you lived in Selfridges?' Whenever he introduces me to anyone, he's always like, 'She's from central London! Did you know there are houses there?'

Stormzy

My mum wanted me to go to Oxford or Cambridge so badly. I got the best GCSE grades in my school, and was given this award because of it. I went to a Harris Academy, so Lord Harris came along to present it to me, and he said, 'If you want to go to Oxford or Cambridge, I will make it happen.' My mum was gassed, everyone was clapping. But I didn't go. A levels were too much for me. I didn't feel it.

Kaylum

I first started to realise I could make a living from videos when I was young. Maybe aged fourteen or fifteen. I used to bunk off school to make videos. I was one of them people. And it was around then that I clocked. This could be my life. I thought: In a couple of years, I could actually live off it.

That's when I decided not to focus on education. I used to take media studies in school – but I was just being taught stuff that I could already do. Some of the stuff on YouTube I learned when I was very young. At that time, age sixteen, I had to stay in education, so I made an agreement with my school to drop out, and went to a college in King's Cross, for five hours a week, instead. That's it. I wasn't learning anything.

At that time, at Link Up, I was making videos for a lot of up-and-coming artists like Section Boyz and Yungen. But no one knew who I was! As soon as I turned sixteen, I just thought: Now I can go fully in.

Tobe

I can't really remember when I first met Mike. I grew up in Peckham, but my mum moved us to Croydon when I was in secondary school. His sister is my age, so a lot of her friends and people that she went to primary school with were my friends, and I think I first heard about him or met him that way. He was starting to rap and posting videos online. This was back when YouTube gained popularity, and he was getting a couple of thousand views, which at that time was big. It was quite exciting seeing people you knew on YouTube, but when I first heard about him, I just thought: OK, so Pinky's little brother raps now. At that time, if people were rapping, everyone was always saying, 'Yeah, man, you can blow!' and not really mean it. But I remember watching one of his freestyles with my friend, and just being like, 'Wait, play that again. He's talking sense! This is sick!' I really felt a conviction that there was something special about him, immediately. I just felt like he could do it. This guy can be more than what I'm seeing. The music thing might work.

We met a little while after that. It might have been at a friend's house. I just remember going up to him and saying, 'You're sick!' It's not the kind of thing you'd normally say, but I just couldn't control it. So I got home and saw that he'd friended me on Facebook, and it went from there. We lived one road away from each other, so we started to meet up and talk about things. We gelled in our similarities. We were both doing quite well academically, both ambitious. I remember discussing things that kids that age don't really discuss.

Stormzy

We know where we're from. We're from a place where no one is coming to help us. The government isn't coming to help us.

No one is coming to help us. We know as young black people from the ends that we are at a disadvantage. We've known that for a long time. And if you know that, and you come from it, don't continue it. Break the cycle.

2.

Alec (Twin)

Me and my brother went to college in south London, so we started playing a few parties and club nights down there. We never properly locked anything down on radio though. And after college I took a year out before university, working in marketing and accounting, just spending my days watching videos online and thinking about DJing on the weekend. I was DJing wherever I could. I didn't think a career in music was really a possibility, but I wasn't sure exactly what else I'd be doing. It was such an impossible thing.

I started uni and me and my brother tried to keep up the music, too. In fact, we started our own production company, making mixtapes in a studio back east.

One day we decided to put together a mixtape of hip hop and grime. On the tape we had Lethal B, Donae'o, Durrty Goodz, So Solid, Estelle, D Double E, J2K, Klashnekoff. All exclusive freestyles. The only person who didn't come along was Major Ace, and he was the person I'd known the longest. We went to an MTV event and Ras Kwame was there, who had a show on 1Xtra, and I gave him a copy of the CD. The next day I got a call from his producer, asking if we could come in to talk about how it came to be. So me, my brother and Crisis went on his show to talk about it, and afterwards the producer called me back up and said they thought I sounded good on air, and asked if I would come back to make a pilot. So I did, and they gave me a show. This was like a week after I got the job at Ministry.

It was an important time for British music as a whole. I don't think anyone really knew how important it was. I was an R&B and hip hop fan, so for me, having Ludacris, Jay-Z and Beenie Man playing alongside Dizzee, Estelle and Fallacy & Fusion, in the daytime, on a mainstream radio station, was important. It was something that wasn't happening that much even on pirate radio. To present the UK artists alongside international artists helped people take UK music seriously, I think. And it was good to be a part of that. Dizzee and Kano were just as good as any artists coming out of the US. But the US artists were always taken so much more seriously. We had our own superstars, we were making amazing music, we just didn't have the infrastructure or the history to really break through. Our generation had very little support . . . But you could feel it was changing. The UK garage scene didn't back grime, UK hip hop felt like a completely different world and wasn't always that welcoming to some of the new things that were happening in UK MC culture.

It felt like 1Xtra was kind of like a reset button. It was the start of 'something'. We were embracing UK underground culture, and embracing those artists as real artists: Dizzee, Kano, Klashnekoff, MC Sway. And it was nationwide. It was bigger than London. I joined a couple of years after it started.

I always felt lucky to be there. I grew up listening to a lot of the artists they were playing, so it was all very serious. I just wanted to keep playing, and talk about the music with passion and knowledge. I cared. These were artists whose careers I had followed from early. I felt like I had a responsibility to know as much as possible about the tracks I was playing, but I also knew some of the artists personally. I grew with the success of the scene. So when Tinchy Stryder became a pop star I was involved. My brother was working with Tinchy on the marketing side, and got a job at Island as a result – he's now President of Urban there! I was DJing for Tinchy on tour. Chip was supporting. And next year Chip had his success. Then it was Tinie Tempah. Then it was Wretch. And these were all people I was connected to.

Austin

I was a fan of music first and foremost, but I never thought I'd ever get a chance to work in music. I was actually leaning towards the film and TV industry initially. I did a bit of work experience, and then got a job in marketing at the BBC, working for Radio 4 and Radio 5 Live. So I was there for six months. Hated it. It was the most boring job ever. The BBC at that time seemed to be very white and very stuffy, and looking back now it was why I probably didn't enjoy working there. It felt mainly made up of Oxbridge graduates and I couldn't really relate to any of my colleagues. It was dinner parties in Richmond versus hanging out on the block with a couple of the mandem. Which is ironic, given the fact that I now get invited to those same dinner parties!

While I was there, a job came up at 1Xtra. The advert said you needed to have good music industry connections, which I thought I kind of did from knowing quite a few people, and you needed to have experience programming for a wide array of audiences, which I sort of did through my job in marketing. I was twenty going on twenty-one, and the job was really for someone with more experience. It wasn't for someone just out of college. I applied on a wing and a prayer, and got an interview. I had to do a music test in a little room – a kind of Trivial Pursuit for black music sounds. This is before the days of Wi-Fi and iPhones, so I couldn't even google the answers! I think I did OK in the test, but it was the interview that got me through. The person interviewing me must have spotted something – a glint in my eye, perhaps – and they offered me the job.

Fraser

I started off as a guitar player, playing in studios and on tour for people like Tony Hadley, Spandau Ballet, Rick Wakeman, and anyone who would take me really, just to pay the rent. I got into producing only because I started to spend more time in the studio, helping to record tracks with pop producers, and slowly got to know what a producer actually was, and what a songwriter was. There wasn't much information available online about particular roles within the industry, so there was no real way to find out unless you were doing it. This was the pre-YouTube days.

I eventually got my own studio, and began to work on some of my own stuff, and that's when I met Craig David. I got to know Craig a little bit, and one day he asked me if I could come along and play guitar on TFI Friday with him. So I did, playing 'Fill Me In', and it seemed to go down well. Then we did Jools Holland together, and a load of TV and radio shows, and it immediately felt like the start of something. Our chemistry was great, and people liked the acoustic aspect – he was reaching a whole new audience. He wasn't just this garage star any more. He was a more rounded artist and singer. And suddenly we found ourselves on this crazy roller coaster of three or four years of working together, and touring the world together, and writing and remixing songs, and we eventually became incredibly close. He was best man at my wedding.

Rachel

I started dance classes when I was five, and kept it up until the age of seventeen or so, when I realised a career in dance wasn't for me. I wasn't really sure what I wanted to do, so I started temping, working in call centres and answering emergency calls. Along with dance my other passion was music. I grew up in a fairly musical household; there was always music blaring out of the speakers in most rooms and my brother has always been a huge hip hop head, and in turn shaped a lot of my own tastes.

At home where I grew up in Bedford, I had a friend whose older brother was a promoter. He organised music events, and used to bring over a lot of big US stars and take them touring around the UK and Europe. I remember saying to him, 'If there's any possibility of doing anything at all with you, even if it's making teas, let me know as I'd love to be involved.' He said, 'Actually, we are looking to expand the team.' So he invited me in for a chat, and said, 'Well, we're looking for an intern for six months.'

Akua

I've always kind of known what I wanted to do. Actually, no: when I was younger, I wanted to work in advertising. Because I loved adverts, and I always thought: Oh, that's clever, or: I wouldn't have put that ending in, and so on. But my first proper job was at Gap, when I was like sixteen, seventeen. And I only got a job at Gap because of the Madonna and Missy Elliott advert. I was like: Well, if they can get Madonna and Missy to work together, then they must be good. It was incredible. I suppose that was where my first idea of brands came from.

After that, I got a job at Selfridges. I was there when the Missy Elliott and Adidas collaboration launched. I arrived at work at 8 a.m. and there were all these boxes everywhere, and people were like, 'Oh yeah, that's the new range,' in a matter-of-fact way. And I remember opening the boxes and just thinking: What. The. Hell. Is. This? It blew my mind. The idea that Missy Elliott could have her own range with Adidas was incredible. I was like: Oh my gosh, Adidas is the coolest brand ever. But it was more than appreciation for what they were doing, it was a sense that I wanted to be a part of it: I have to work there. So then I kind of found my way there as an intern, and the rest is history. The same for football. I just wanted to work in football, so I found a way to get there.

These things are just passions or interests. I've always thought: Oh, that brand is sick. What can I do to work with them? And I've just been super blessed in making those connections, and finding people who've welcomed me.

Austin

When I joined 1Xtra I was fearless – the kind of fearlessness that you look back on and sometimes cringe about. But I'd spent hundreds and hundreds of hours listening to music and burning CDs. I was prepared. When preparation meets luck, that's when amazing things happen.

There were people there who were sceptical of my ability to do the job. A few people who were like: Wait, who's this random twenty-one-year-old with a screw face? But on the whole I was welcomed. It was the new BBC. It was diverse, it was young, it was a sexy mixture of people. I felt welcomed. I dived straight in. The Wretch 32 and Scorcher mixtape, that was my first job. That's what they said when I arrived: 'Go and listen to that.'

I was really lucky in that my boss took me under her wing and gave me more responsibility from day one. So if she was off, I would step in to cover for her. She put me forward to do extra things.

1. preparation

'Flipz said remember
the talks that we had
on the road, and never
lose sight of the dream.'
'Intro', *Dreamer's Disease*.

DJ TiiNY.

Tobe.

Kaylum.

TiiNY at one of the first #Merky shows, Sheffield.

'Wicked Skengman 2'
video, February 2014.

'Went Jools Holland
in my tracksuit, rep
for the scene like
yeah man I had to.'

Preparation with TiiNY.

'We've got ten man chasing a dream.' 'Not That Deep' video, 2014.

Akua.

Trevor in Texa

Live in the flesh.

I'm also a naturally nosy person. I like knowing what's going on. I think that's what has allowed me to stay relevant in this industry. My graffiti name was Mr Views – because I'd give my views on everything, whether people wanted to hear them or not. And at 1Xtra it was the same. I'd speak up in meetings and eventually started getting asked for my opinions about things that were really above my pay grade. I was like: Should I really be in this meeting? Should I be the one to answer that question? But that also led to me asking questions, too. Why are we broadcasting this? Why are we running these events? Why are we only playing this amount of UK music? Why is this artist being supported and this other artist isn't? And I found that when you constantly ask questions, and ask questions in the right way, people become very receptive to you and to your ideas.

Alec (Twin)

In 2007, I also had a label running with Richard Antwi. After Ministry I worked for Sony Publishing briefly, then set up a joint venture project called Levels. The very first project we put out was 'Wearing My Rolex'.

That was a Bless Beats project. I knew Bless Beats from when we were kids. I knew him from church. I knew his mum. So he called me up one day and said, 'Look, I've just made this tune with Wiley, and I think it's big.' I didn't even realise he was producing properly. So I said, 'OK, come to my office and we'll talk about it.' He came in with Wiley and played it. To me, it just sounded like a smash. Instantly. If you marry

Wiley's credibility with a tune like this, a grime record that Pete Tong could play, it could be huge. That weekend Target premiered it, and everything kicked off. Then Pete Tong actually did play it. Suddenly you had every label throwing massive amounts of money at Bless Beats. He came to see me and said, 'Twin, we need to figure out what we're doing here.' I was just starting to talk to Ben Cook at Atlantic about a joint venture, so I called him and we set up a meeting with Wiley, Bless Beats and their lawyer one afternoon. We were stuck in an office for like four hours, thrashing it out.

That was the first grime pop hit. After that Dizzee had his run. Then Tinie. But it was Wiley first. It was a statement of intent. It was him saying, 'If I want to try this pop game, I can.' This is a guy who would spend two hours spitting lyrics on a radio show. For him to produce a track where he's saying like three or four things, and for it to go gold and be a monster hit? Loved that!

Austin

My very first job in the music industry was effectively to programme all of the daytime music on 1Xtra, from six in the morning to seven in the evening. There would always be a wider strategy behind it: 'We've got to support more females.' 'We've got to play more UK music.' This all feeds into the programming. Most radio stations have programming software. Programming was essentially like pressing shuffle on a very large playlist. The programme was divided up into clock hours. You take it hour by hour. So the first few seconds of the first hour will be a jingle. The same jingle every single day. Then you have an A-list record, which is one of our biggest records. Then you've got a C-list record. Then you've got a thirty-second break for the DJ to introduce the next track. And so on. It was my job to set up those clocks, and to decide what went into every single one of those segments. On 1Xtra, you had about 140 songs you could play on any given day. I would try to play the biggest tracks of the moment, but also to make sure that we're dedicating enough time for younger or lesser known artists.

It was amazing. I would come in every morning and be a DJ for the nation. What will people want to listen to at 7 a.m.? Some people will be getting ready for school. Some people will be coming home from work. Some people will already be in the office. The key question was always: How do I capture the biggest swathe of society? I've sat in hundreds of playlist meetings and scheduled over 30,000 hours of radio at the BBC – so I like to think I'm world class in my position! There's basically a generation of people who grew up on the tastes of me and my team, and that feels pretty surreal.

That was the second most influential position on the network, you could argue. I was in that position for four years or so. Then my boss went on maternity leave, so I stepped up into her role for ten months. And then she came back, and I was put back in my old role, and, like most young people would, I had a bit of a hissy fit and left the BBC. But I had been really spoiled. My first job in music was at the end of the conveyor belt, in a very influential position. I have always liked to challenge myself, so I thought: You know what?

Maybe it's time to grow as a leader. So I teamed up with an investor, and I started up a talent management agency, looking after DJs and artists, and some athletes, and also did a bit of consultancy for the major labels. I did that for two years, and then I got headhunted by the BBC. My old boss had handed in her notice, so they wanted me to come back and be the music manager. I felt quite happy coming back. I was put forward for the BBC's senior management programme, I was picked as one of *Music Week*'s '30 Under 30' list. Things were good.

Rachel

I had no idea what I was doing – but I was hungry to learn and to absorb what was going on and just involved myself in everything. I ended up staying for a year. Although I was hugely grateful for the opportunity, I wanted more and I couldn't see how I could grow there. I must have applied to hundreds of jobs at various record labels, and as expected, didn't receive a single reply. Then a friend said, 'What about start-ups? There's a lot of smaller music companies getting going, and just doing their own thing.' Again, I had no real idea about any of this, but I signed up to Twitter and discovered a whole new world of possibilities. There were so many young entrepreneurs and creatives online, and it was a little easier to make contact with them. So I did.

Stormzy

I didn't come from nowhere. It's impossible for someone to come from nowhere.

The old-school Channel U foundation played a massive part in opening my eyes to what could be done, by just showing me stars in the hood. It was that basic level of knowing that man from man's ends can be successful, in some way, shape or form, from Dizzee and Wiley onwards. Then you had the next generation – Chip, Tinchy Stryder, Devlin, Wretch 32. These were people on television, wearing tracksuits, sponsored by Adidas. They may be from London, but it's someone else's ends. The only difference was that it was never south. When I was a young, ambitious, budding spitter, aged twelve or thirteen, all you really had from south was Southside Allstars. For me, Bow E3 was the promised land. If you're from Bow, your elders are Nasty Crew and Roll Deep. It's something else.

The big moment came with Krept & Konan. They were the mandem. There's probably a psychological term for it. Up to that point I loved the music, and I've got so much respect for the people who came before me, but I wasn't really being inspired. We were just kids listening to the greasiest shit. That all changed when I heard Krept & Konan.

Tobe

I've always been ambitious. I've always thought, if you're going to do something, you might as well do it as well as you can do.

I've never left a job until I've gone as far as I can. And I was always the friend who spurred him on. I knew from very early how to take things to the next stage. Rather than making a freestyle just for us, why not film it properly, put it on YouTube, see what happens? You don't even need to make a sick video, people just need to see you rapping.

Our business ethos was established before the music career took off. I remember sitting in a friend's house when we were young, just talking about how we were going to make money. It was a time when the first of our friends were going to jail. We saw so many friends lose so much of their childhood because they wanted more. It wasn't that we were super-good boys, but we weren't naive. We knew that if it happened to them, it could happen to us. We knew we had to find a way to establish ourselves without breaking the law.

We were sitting down talking about event organising and other things. It started with eleven friends saying, 'Yes, let's do it. Let's make it happen.' A couple of weeks later it was just me and Stormzy. Still actively trying to find a way to do something greater. This was 2011 or 2012.

As the years went by Stormzy started taking music seriously, but he was also doing other things. Music was kind of secondary. School or college or work came first. He was always the guy who used to come along and drop a freestyle, but it was more of a hobby. It was only when he got the engineering role that he realised how unfulfilling it was. He had regular money, and he could support his mum a little bit, but he wasn't happy. He wasn't satisfied. He felt like he was missing out.

Music started to become more of a focus. Our conversations became more music-oriented. The question became how he could grow within music. So I'd research, speak to people, show him things. I was into hip hop so I'd be looking at what was happening in hip hop – what was happening in the US, or what other artists were doing – and talk to him about it. And every time we met the conversation grew.

Stormzy

I've known Flipz for a long time. He was always my bredrin, but I didn't have his number or anything. It was mad cool. His big brother and my big sister were friends. I'd see him every once in a while but that was about it. And then I got stabbed. I was lying down, my head in my girl's lap, and I remember Flipz just pushing his way through the crowd and looking at me and saying, 'Bro, you cool?' and I said, 'Yeah, bro, I'm good.' He just kissed his teeth and walked off. Funny how life works, innit? When he saw me bleeding on the floor and I saw him peering over neither of us could've ever imagined being right here on this journey together. Imagine that.

I can't tell you when we first started rolling, but at some point we did. Maybe from 2012 or thereabouts. We were just out here. We came up. I remember being dead broke with this guy and him having to bail me out of bare embarrassing situations. One time I was with this girl, just driving round the ends trying to smooth talk her, and my petrol light came on. I knew that I could break down any minute, so I drove down to Flipz's, with the girl in my passenger seat, and then he came down and we had a brief fake chat about whatever to distract the girl from the trickery that was about to happen. After the fake chat he shook my hand and slipped me £50 to go fill up my tank. Mission complete.

Flipz

We are all from the same area. Stormzy went to Harris Academy, just down the road, and I went to St Joseph's. My older brother and his older sister were very close. So we linked up. He used to rap, used to spit with my cousin. We were just rolling around together.

By 2011, 2012, we were both kind of doing our thing. I was working, and he was doing his engineering apprenticeship, up in Southampton. He put out the 168 mixtape and was getting some good feedback, but he was working. He couldn't do both.

And then one day he turned up at my house in a suit and said that he'd quit his job.

Rachel

I then met a guy called Austin. I was familiar with him from his time at BBC Radio 1Xtra, and had heard through the grapevine that he was starting up a music company called The Hub. It was predominantly a management company, but with PR and radio plugging arms as well. I saw he'd tweeted saying that he was looking for interns, so I emailed him, and he replied asking if I could come and meet him that day. So I hopped on a train and went and met him on a bench outside Starbucks in Angel, and we just chatted and walked around, and he said, 'OK, can you come and start as an intern next week?' So I did. Austin's a great guy and always willing to help, especially if someone is looking to get a foot in the door in music somehow.

It was a brand-new company, and there was no one on the PR side at all when I joined. In a nutshell, it was my job to go out and find talent, ask them to sign up to The Hub, and run their PR campaigns. That's actually also where I first met (my now wonderful friend) Twin B; The Hub had just secured a Sennheiser headphone campaign for him and I had to help on the PR for it.

It was fun, and fairly high-pressured. I had a lot of targets to hit, and being quite new to PR, this was all very new to me. Initially, I spent a lot of time studying other companies and campaigns to get a better understanding of what was possible. I quickly realised that so much of your success in PR depends on your relationship with journalists and the projects you are attached to. That's really how you get noticed in the industry; that's how people see you. I was at an amazing brand-new company that was doing really well, but I was working on a lot of projects I sadly wasn't really that passionate about, just to ensure I met my targets. I couldn't just conjure up the kind of passion you need to get people to pay attention, and I felt journalists were starting to realise.

Akua

It took me ten years to find my feet at Adidas. Every day was a new day.

Then 2012 was a big moment. Adidas was a principal sponsor of the Olympic Games, so we knew it was coming. It was something the business had been working on for six years or so; the work starts that far in advance. And as it got closer, everyone was dreading it. We couldn't wait for it to be over. I think most of the country felt the same, actually. Until the opening ceremony. And then our whole opinion of the Games just changed. London was amazing, and the sun was out, and the glow that came over the city was crazy, and the Olympics just changed everything.

That was probably one of the toughest stints. We had a base in St Paul's, where we had a suite, where we could invite artists to pick up tickets and gifts, and we'd take them to various events. And we had the Village Underground, where there was programming going on every single day. So I'd spend the day in St Paul's, then walk down to Village Underground where I'd stay until two o'clock in the morning, and then walk over to a little hotel in Hoxton where I lived for a few weeks. It was the same every day. Get up in the morning and go to St Paul's, then go to Village Underground, and back to Hoxton and so on. And meanwhile the office was still running as normal because life was still happening. It was just the most exhausting period, and amazing. But after that I realised I'd done all I'd really wanted to do.

I decided to go back to university, so I was studying part-time and working full-time, and then I took a sabbatical, because I just needed to work out what I wanted to do next. When I came back Adidas said, 'You can take on the Rita Ora project,' and I was so excited, but a couple of months in I just thought: No, I don't want to do this any more.

It's a really weird one, because I didn't leave on a downer. I left an incredible team that I still miss. I still miss being in that unit. But at the same time, I felt: Well, I just want to work on the things that I want to work on. I want to have the ability to say, 'Yes, I want to do that,' or 'No, I don't want to do that.' And I just thought: I have to do it now. What am I going to do? Wait until I'm forty-five? I have to do it now. And if it doesn't work out, God forbid, I'll just find another job, I'll start filling in application forms. I made peace with it. Even if it's only six months and at the end I'm broke and no one wants to work with me, then so be it.

It was always the brand first, as well. That's usually how it works. Like, Wretch will always remember our 2012 campaign. That's a thing for us. Or Rita will always remember our campaign. But it's not me, it's Adidas. Regardless of what you've done, it feels a little bit like your identity has been stripped away from you.

From the day I decided to leave right through to the day I actually left for the last time, I didn't think I could do it for myself. I had nothing concrete there waiting for me. All I had was some ideas and some numbers of people that I was going to call. And that's the truth of it, really.

DJ TiiNY

Not many people are putting in the time and effort from an early age. Everyone's just trying to get things their way. I started young. I was DJing when I was fourteen. This is Channel U days.

I got a lot of offers quickly. There were parties every weekend. I was going to all these areas, and thinking: Is this going to be OK? Every day was a challenge. Is the party going to be peak, or is someone going to get jerked? Back then, if you were our age, and more so if you were a bit older, like sixteen or seventeen, certain parts of south London were sticky. Guys were mad. We were glad to make it home.

I was a younger, and I was looking at all these olders. I didn't think there was anyone in my generation who was going to help me. Now I see a lot of young black people doing their thing, Kenny Allstar, P Montana, Cosmic and all these man. Back then, there wasn't really anyone. I was trying to study, and see how I could pattern. Is it just me? Do I just DJ at house parties? I wanted to be someone's DJ. I was trying to get in touch with people at Choice FM, Kiss, BBC. I didn't really know what I was doing. I just thought: I've got to email people. And surprisingly, I got an answer. I did my first guest mix when I was fifteen, on Choice FM. I was doing all sorts. I was doing house parties, club bookings. I had a friend up in Leicester at university so I was doing a lot up there.

I was in a bit of a bubble. It was all De Montfort raves and bar crawls and that. I was in Year 10 at this point, so I'd go up on a Friday with my cousins, Saturday the rave was on. I was fifteen but I was lanky so I'd just cut through.

Kaylum

People respect videos more now. When I was fifteen or sixteen, no one really cared. Music is a lot more important to the culture than the visuals. It's a lot bigger in the US. More people know me in America than know me here, weirdly. Our music scene and our visual scene are separate. Up to a couple of years ago, a producer wouldn't get credited. Young up-and-coming producers wouldn't get noticed because they weren't allowed to tag their videos.

I'll be real with you: when I was at Link Up, I was shooting videos and editing videos, but that was about it. You're not really around the artists. You do the video and that's it. I thought that producing content for a media platform was the biggest goal. It's only when I started hanging out with Stormzy and a few others in the industry who were helping me along my way that I began to see things differently. Video is something I love, but I also love trying new things. He said to me, 'Forget Kaylum Link Up – think about Kaylum Dennis.' I could do a lot more.

Fraser

It got to a point when I felt I needed to forge my own way. I decided one day that from that point on, I was going to stop touring, because it was really taking it out of me musically. No more guitar playing. I needed to do my own thing. So I went back home and converted the spare room of my flat in Acton into a studio, and started from there.

From working with Craig, I had managed to build up quite a good network of contacts, and had a publishing deal myself, so I had enough to be getting on with. One of the people I'd got to know was Richard Thomas, Kano's manager. He called me up one day and asked if I'd be interested in working with Kano. They were looking for a guitar player, and he knew I played and also produced, so he came in. On the first day we made 'Typical Me'.

Up to that point, Kano had been in with a lot of really good grime producers: DaVinChe, Mikey J, Terror Danjah, but I think I brought something a bit different, musically. I could pick up a guitar, or add something unexpected, like the Elgar string sample on 'Signs in Life'.

We worked with quite a few grime legends around that time. I remember Ghetts used to come into the studio with Kano, taking the train from Canning Town to Acton, through Willesden, Harlesden and that way. And there would always be some drama on the way, but the work we were doing obviously meant enough to them to make the trip from east to west London.

Manon

I studied audio engineering in France and moved to the UK to find work – and also because all the music I liked came from the UK or the US. French music is great, but it wasn't what I was listening to, growing up. I moved over, and started working in studios as a freelance engineer, and then I met Fraser. He asked me to help him in the studio for a while, and it all kind of went from there. If someone told me ten years ago that I would have been working on grime tracks in the UK then I wouldn't have believed them.

Trevor

I've been running my own tour company for eight years, but I got into it by mistake, near enough. My background was in IT and sales. But I was also singing in a choir, and then a bit later, running that choir. And very quickly, alongside everything else I was doing, the choir started to take off. Soon we were singing on X Factor, singing before European Cup matches, and starting to put on our own shows across Europe and that kind of thing. I managed all our tours, so I was in effect a tour manager, but I also had my day job. Eventually I had to step back from the choir because it was taking over.

The one thing that always wound me up at that time was going to concerts and just seeing everything being put together quite shabbily. Nothing was properly thought through, nothing was running on time, everything was just a bit basic. I kept on moaning about it, but suddenly thought, instead of complaining, why not just do my own thing?

So I started a night called Souled Out in Hackney and Brixton with my good friend David in live music venues rather than church venues to reach a wider audience. I ran everything properly. Everything started on time, first and foremost. Artists would get vexed, because I'd say, 'You're on,' and there would be five people or so in the audience. After a while the audience got to know. The show started at seven thirty. And at seven thirty the venue was completely packed. Souled Out was a big success, in the church community and in the local community, and it got to the stage where artists were asking me to run their own shows for them.

I was working full-time at this stage, and I really had no life. But it took me about a year and a half to pluck up the courage to make the leap. I gave myself a year – If it doesn't work out in a year, I'll just go back to what I was doing. I had a few shows going on. I had plenty to be getting on with.

There was one night when everything changed. I was asleep and my phone started ringing constantly. This is like 2 a.m. Eventually I picked up and it was a friend of mine who looked after live performances for various artists. He was like, 'Trev! I need you to come and manage this show.' I said, 'OK, calm down. No trouble.' And he said, 'No, you don't understand! We need you here at 8 a.m.' It was the MTV 'Brand New' show: Wretch 32, Tinie Tempah and Labrinth. This was just before they all took off. So I went in and worked with him on the show and by God's grace all went well.

After that, my friend asked if I'd like to come and help with production on Tinie's live shows, which I was happy to do. Around that time I was introduced to Wretch's team as his new tour manager – a job I didn't even know existed – and we started talking about what they needed to be done. It was everything I used to do with my choir. So I was basically tour managing for a long time and not even realising that was what I was doing.

From there things really started snowballing.

Akua

I brought Stormzy into Adidas and I just knew it was going to work. We'd decided to invest in him. But no one could have foreseen what was going to happen. No one could have seen what was coming next. His trajectory was crazy.

Flipz

Stormzy's always been good. He's highly blessed. Even in terms of school, he could easily have gone to Oxford.

When he quit his job he was living with no money. It was really show to show, getting petrol money and on to the next thing. It showed me that he really wanted it.

The freestyles were mad. He'd just phone us and say, 'Right, White Horse Estate,' or, 'Purley Tesco,' and everyone would go there. Even if it was raining. His cameraman at the time would record it, and he'd be on at him to edit it and get it out as quickly as possible.

Tobe

Take 168, one of his first ever mixtapes: 168 is the number of hours in seven days. He only had a seven-day break from his engineering course, and so seven days to record the mixtape. It was good, but it could have been better. It was frustrating, because I could see how good it could have been if he wasn't restricted by his work. He was being held back. I could see what might be possible if he had the freedom and time to just make music.

I wasn't his manager at this point. I was only a friend who wanted him to win. But when he made 168, I knew there were certain things that needed to change. I

could see that people would invest in him if he invested
in himself.

Flipz

If you grow up where we grew up, you're trapped, and
you don't even know it. What are you aiming for? I didn't
know what was possible. My parents wanted the best for
me, but they couldn't tell me what to do. My teachers
couldn't tell me what to do. You either figure it out for
yourself, or you don't.

If you're good, you've just got to be able to share your talent
with people. Make a tune, record a video, post it on YouTube,
and you're there. Man can eat off that. You've just got to get it
out there.

That's why I'm always happy to help talented youngers.
If they've got talent, and there's something I can do to help
them, I will. It's courage as well. It takes a bit of courage to
reach out. But what have you got to lose? Believe in yourself.
People will pay attention if you're good, and you've put in the
work. A lot of man are stuck, and they've just got to figure a
way out.

Stormzy

There's a power in knowing where home is. They pray for me,
they pray for me hard. It's like, my mum spends most of her
time praying for me. I ran off into the world like: Shit, I've got
to go get it, I've got to go get it for everyone.

3.

Stormzy

Back in the day, it was all about making a tune, shooting a video, getting it up on YouTube. YouTube videos were my bread and butter back then. They still are now, don't get me wrong, but that was all we had back then.

Flipz

The team started off slowly. I remember us having a meeting at a shisha spot in Norbury. It was me, Stormz, Jaiden, his cameraman at the time, and a close friend called Ninny. A couple black brothers and girl just putting it together. And he basically spelled out exactly what was going to happen, and said that we just needed to be patient. We were all sitting there listening to him, nodding our heads. It's all happened.

Austin

For us, we always supported the artists who were really trying. Off the top of my head, I could probably name around fifty artists today who have got a strong team around them, and a real structure, and are making money and touring and all of that. And I could probably name another 150 who haven't quite got the full team, but are still doing their thing. It was completely different when I started. This was when grime was going through a bit of a recession. The era of Dizzee and Wiley was ending, and we were a bit of a way off the next wave coming through. I mean, I joined at the worst possible moment for black British music.

There were many reasons for it. The structure of the British media wasn't really set up to support black British sounds at that time. You've got to think about it in simple terms. How many black faces, or how many diverse faces, or how many people who understood diversity were in positions of influence? Who was programming *Top of the Pops*? Who was editing the *Sun* or the *Evening Standard*? Maybe you had people who didn't quite understand diversity in the way that the people who are in similar positions today do. And as an industry, we didn't have enough business minds on the back end. On the front end, you had a hell of a lot of talent, but in the back end, there just weren't enough people who were happy and able to be in the background and operate the machinery. It's no coincidence that the moment that changed, the moment you had people like Tobe come to the fore, at the same time as you had people like me in positions of influence in companies like the BBC, amazing things happened. When I started, though, things were not good.

But what I can say, quite proudly, is that me and the 1Xtra team fought really hard to bring it back up again. Supporting artists like Chip, Tinie Tempah, Tinchy Stryder, Kano. And these aren't artists that we made, but artists that we tried to put in front of the world. When I look back, I think: Yeah, we really did our thing. We launched events like 1Xtra Live, at a time when it was unheard of to launch an arena tour with UK artists. We even took it to Wembley! It was super exciting. And as you see one artist take off, you see another come into view.

Alec (Twin)

At some point in 2013 or 2014, I think, someone tweeted a video of a Stormzy freestyle. Maybe one of the 'Wicked Skengman' videos. I can't remember exactly which one it was, because after watching it I stayed up for hours trying to find every video of his on the Internet, watching videos on my phone, then switching on my laptop at 2 a.m. and trawling through YouTube. This was just before you had Meridian Dan's 'German Whip', and Skepta's re-emergence. It wasn't necessarily a stale moment in British MC culture, but it felt like a moment when something new needed to happen. Someone exciting to shake it up a bit. I didn't actually realise it until I watched those videos.

I found him captivating. That moment when he drops his brow, I just thought he was going to jump out of the screen and slap me with a lyric. You could see he was a leader as well. Even if there were other people on the screen, he was the centre of everything. He was versatile, too. There was a video of him *singing* at a show.

I followed him on Twitter and then I just watched him and became a fan. He was one of a few of a new bunch of MCs coming through like Novelist and others, and I'd often stay up until 2 a.m. watching freestyles on YouTube. His always grabbed me, entertained me, kept me. He had it.

I really wanted to meet him, but I also wanted to meet him at the right time. Atlantic had just moved offices. I was wary of speaking to him too soon, if that makes any sense. I knew there was something special about him, but I wondered how much he thought of himself as an artist. There were things he was doing that really showed sniffs of that. How seriously he was taking it. Walking into a label can be a daunting thing. Sometimes I feel that if I meet an artist too early it might not be the right time. One thing I've come to realise is I've never approached my job as a job. It's just an extension of a passion and a skill set that I've developed. I have to remind myself that for a lot of artists, having a meeting with a label can be a point of arrival of sorts. I don't like that side of things, because I think it can take away from being able to build with a person, because of the situation you connect in. If I approach an artist, just by the nature of my job, it's not always a natural conversation. Which is a shame, because I like meeting new artists. But with Stormz it was natural from the get-go.

I can't remember why or when he first came in – I think

it might have been via Sian Anderson – but he came in one day for a meeting. He was so tall, and he was rich in his complexion. I can remember he just started laughing a bit, and sat down in a chair in my office, and let out a big sigh. His tracksuit bottoms rode up a bit. And he spotted some of the plaques on the wall, in particular the Ed Sheeran one and started asking loads of questions. We spoke for about two or three hours, him just bombarding me with questions. And I did the same to him.

I was working on Wretch 32's new album at the time, and we spoke a lot about Wretch, and the fact that we both saw him as a writer as much as a rapper. '6 Words' had just come out, and I was still amazed by it, and the fact that he had the confidence to release a track where he didn't rap, although for me he's one of the most talented rappers on the planet. We talked loads about how he got to that point as an artist, and how success can lead to that confidence, and that artistry. We just hit it off. I thought he was one of the most interesting human beings I've ever met. And he's easily one of the most intelligent people I've ever met.

Austin

The first time I heard Stormzy's name was on my way to work. I get a train that's packed full of kids from a local secondary school, and I heard his name a couple of times, but didn't really know who he was. Then I had dinner with a manager, and he said, 'Have you heard of this guy Stormzy? He's this kid from south London who's causing a lot of fuss.' It sort of clicked, but

I just put it into my memory bank. I am told about so many new artists every day, so I just stored it away and didn't really think anything of it. Then a couple of days later I saw my nephew, who's one of my main A&R sources, and he was fifteen at the time, in 2014 or so, and he said, 'Uncle, are 1Xtra playing Stormzy?' And I said, 'OK, this is the third time I've heard this boy's name. Something's going on.'

I googled him, and watched a couple of his videos, and by the third, I was like: OK, cool, I'm going to reach out to this guy. So I found him on Twitter, and at this time he had about 800 followers, and we followed each other, and I sent him a message. One thing I noticed at the time was that although he only had 800 followers or so, he was still getting thirty, forty and fifty retweets on every single tweet. Other artists with hundreds of thousands of followers weren't getting that kind of response. It was surprising. So I heard back from him, and I invited him into the studio. I remember it so clearly. The meeting was at two o'clock, and he turned up at one fifty-five. And as soon as he walked into the studio, I knew I was dealing with a star.

Flipz

Akua was one of the first, back when she was working with Adidas. She worked with everyone back then, but she saw something different in Stormzy. The first time we went there, I was wearing my Air Force 1s, but they gave us loads of clothes anyway. Adidas came through, and then a lot of other companies got in touch. Supermalt delivered a few crates to his mum's house. She was gassed!

Akua

Ayesha is friends with one of my younger cousins so I've known her for a long time. Of the team, though, I got to know Stormzy first. He used to come to the Adidas office and leave Flipz downstairs in the car, because they were parked on double yellows. So I heard Flipz's name before I met him, but then he started coming to the office too. And then Tobe next, maybe. I remember having a conversation with Stormzy about managers, and we spoke about the people he was meeting, and he said, 'Well, I've got a friend who's mad smart, I might just go with him,' and I said, 'Do it.'

Austin

At that time, lots of 'established' managers were hollering at Stormzy and offering him all sorts of deals. I mentioned to him that sometimes the best managers can be your friend – just someone who is presentable and understands how to network. Then he called me one day and was like, 'I've got a friend who works for Land Rover – he's really smart, he's good at networking, blah blah blah . . . What do you think?' I gave him my opinion – and I'm sure he asked others for their opinion too. When he decided to go with Tobe and I met him for the first time I knew he had made the right decision. The combination of Stormzy and Tobe is a massive part of the reason he's been able to achieve what he has.

My main belief is that to achieve success, you have to have a team around you who buy in to your vision. And if you have a manager who isn't someone like you, who isn't from your culture, or from your area, then that shared vision is weakened. And by the time it filters through agents or radio or your record label, it's weakened even more. You need to understand the person you're working with. And Tobe does that innately. They're more or less the best of friends. And you add to that Tobe's understanding, his professionalism, his ability to communicate and interface with people like myself, and you get a winning combination. They smashed it as a duo. The things that they were able to achieve even at the start of the journey surprised me.

One of the reasons they trusted me, I think, is that I didn't really have an agenda. My only agenda is to break as many artists as possible, so me and my team look as good as possible. There was a moment when he was white hot on Kensington High Street, for example. They had offers from every major label. And I said to them, 'Look, nothing lasts for ever. You might not want to do a deal now, but you should think about doing a deal soon.' Thank God they didn't listen to me! But I did hook up that meeting with Akua and Adidas, and other things. I tried to be a mentor in some way.

Tobe

It came at a key moment. Stormzy had done so much at that point. He needed someone who could take it to the next level. Logically you would have thought the best thing to do would be to get an established manager, someone with the right connections and experience. It was so strange. Looking back it makes sense, but it was strange at the time.

I was working for Land Rover in Mayfair at the time, but I saw a lot of him, and wanted to help out. I remember we were driving back from central London one day with his sister Rachel and he just turned to me and said, 'Would you want to do the management thing?'

I felt he was giving me an opportunity that I would have to fight for years within any company to get. I can't speak for him, but I think he thought, regardless of what I'd done or hadn't done, I could do this, if I was given the right tools, and had some good people to learn from. I handed in my notice two days after that.

I was ambitious. But it was also him understanding that we could do this. He took a chance, and I'm just someone who welcomes a challenge.

Alec (Twin)

We've been cool since day one, but the dynamic of me being at a label and Stormzy being the hottest unsigned act was funny. He was also unmanaged for a while after I met him. I actually approached a few big management companies to see if they were interested at one point. I thought it would be a statement of intent. I genuinely believed that he would be a megastar, so I thought the obvious thing to do for him would be to find a big manager. If you've got the same manager as, say, a huge pop group, it says something. But it didn't work out. I remember talking to Stormzy about his smartest friend.

A week or so later he called me up and said, 'Bruv, my bredrin is going to come and see you, just to chat.' Tobe came to see me in his suit because he came directly from his graduate job at a big car company, I think. I immediately thought he was a G as well. Smart, honest, knowledgeable and sincere. The next week it was decided. He was forming his team.

Stormzy

I can't lie, when I look back on my career I think I've made a lot of good decisions. Take Tobe, for example. I was so sure of that decision. At the time I was bubbling. I was the hot new thing in music, and I was doing what a hot new thing was supposed to do. I was up and down Kensington High Street a lot at the time, speaking to some highly respected, very successful people. The music industry looked at me and said, 'OK, we think you're ready to come in.' But I wasn't sure if I *was* ready, or what I was supposed to come in to. I had no idea what was going on. But nothing was really sitting right with me, and I knew it had to sit right.

So many of my decisions are down to intuition. Intuition is important in music, as I expect it is in a lot of creative industries. It's like when you hear a song. You can be very scientific in the way you analyse it, and point out exactly how particular elements work and why they work, and which boxes the song ticks, and so on and so forth. But it's also a spiritual thing: you just know it's good.

At the same time I was talking to Tobe a lot, on the block. I'd have these meetings, and then go back to the estate and go to my bredrin's house and bun a zoot. I was always the smartest out of my friendship group, growing up. For sixteen or seventeen years, I was the person who people looked to for answers. And then Tobe came along. I've known Tobe for years, but we only started hanging out properly after the school years. When we did, I thought: Fucking hell, this brother's smarter than me! He was schooling us. He was showing us the ropes, and feeding us so much knowledge. So when I started getting into music, I was always asking him for advice, or getting his feedback on what was happening.

It was never that I felt like I needed a team around, or that I even had a clear idea about what I was doing. We got about eleven or twelve people together one day and talked about #Merky, and what we could do, but it didn't really go anywhere. A lot of people couldn't see it, or couldn't be involved because of what was going on with them. Tobe and I kept talking. We both could see what it could become.

And then one day we were in the car, Tobe was in the front seat, my sister was driving, and I was in the back. He was leaning over, telling me something, and I said, 'Bruv, you should be my manager, you know.' I make it sound like a spontaneous decision, but it was something I'd thought about for a while. It felt right. Even if I had Justin Bieber's manager or Kanye West's manager approach me, I still think I would have made the same decision. He was the best thing for my career. He's young, he's hungry, he's super intelligent, he's a natural leader. The one thing he didn't have was knowledge about the industry, and how it works. But I knew that he had the will to find out, and I knew that he could learn. Easily. To be honest, we could have been doing anything – starting a restaurant, or a tech start-up, or anything. Regardless of what it was, he would have worked it out.

The other thing we share is foresight. I don't like to call it vision, because I don't think vision means very much. But foresight is clear. Seeing something before it happens. And we both had that. A lot of people didn't have the foresight, and that's OK. Foresight is a blessing, and not everyone has it.

DJ TiiNY

I got to college, and by this point I knew Stormzy through a mutual friend. He'd gone to my college but left a couple of years before. His lot were all my brother's friends. So we were in the area, in the same place. But I was just a younger, just DJing. He was the most talked about in the area, from the time he dropped the 168 mixtape. He was smashing it. Everyone thought he was wavy.

And then we did a show in Old Kent Road. My bredrin was like, 'You know he needs someone to play for him.' I thought: Oh, that's calm, but I'll concentrate on my set and see what happens. The place was mad. And after I'd finished my set, he came on after and just gave me these two CDs. So I put them in and started playing. He was spraying bars and everything was going well. Everyone was gassed. Then I started mixing, and it just went mad. Stormzy was gassed, and Tobe was gassed – he was standing at the side of the stage. So after the show Tobe and Stormzy said they'd shout me, and that was it for a while.

I linked up with Stormzy a couple of months after that Old Kent Road show. They said, 'Do you want to DJ for Stormz?' I just thought: Why not go for it? I didn't ask for anything. I just thought: I'm going to do this, and if you lot need me I'm there. If you man reward me then cool, but I'm doing my own thing as well, because I wanted to be a big-name DJ too. I was trying to go HAM with DJing too, trying to enter into new fields. But I thought it could be a blessing.

Stormzy

Back when I was starting out, a good friend of mine was putting on raves, and organising a lot of shows on the university circuit and all of that. This was 2014 and 2015, and no MCs were getting booked. If you were BBK you were OK. That was about it. Grime wasn't dead, but there wasn't much going on. When I put out 'Wicked Skengman 1', '2' and '3', no one was really doing grime.

I was getting by, doing university shows with my friend, just freestyling over classic grime instrumentals. We used to all go up together, like seven-car convoys, thirty man walking into the rave. I had a DJ, but he was a bit unreliable. I have very high standards when it comes to music. I demand a high standard from myself, and from everyone I'm working with. I was just as serious back then as I am today. If someone is bringing me down, or getting in the way of me doing something the way I need it to be done, I won't have it. Some of them have a name for me, 'Smoky Mike', when I get vexed and I tell them off. But it's important to me. Anyway, we were all going up to a show on Old Kent Road one night, and meeting at the yard before we left, getting ready. My DJ turns up, and he's forgotten the CDs. It hadn't been a good day for me, for one reason or another, and I just lost it: 'How could you forget the fucking CDs? You're supposed to be my DJ!' I wasn't having it. My shit needed to be cold. I just said, 'Bruv, you're not DJing for me ever again. That's it.'

Meanwhile, for weeks this friend had been telling me to work with a DJ he knew, TiiNY. I didn't buy it. You're just trying to bust your bredrin. But he wouldn't give up. He was telling me again and again and again. So that night, after my DJ left, I called him up and got TiiNY's number. I said, 'Listen, can you DJ CDs?' He said yes. 'Can you meet us on the Old Kent Road in a couple of hours?' He said yes. So now twenty man are frantically trying to remember all the tunes we need, 'Havana', 'Pied Piper', 'Nutty Violinz', and managed to burn them all onto two CDs. When we got to the rave, TiiNY was waiting. I gave him the two CDs, said, 'Yeah, DJ for man tonight.' He *fucked it up*. He had one shot, and he didn't miss. He badded it up so much that everyone was pulling and pushing him afterwards. I was like, 'All right, you're my DJ.'

It was a similar story with Kaylum. The first time he came on board, I had asked someone else to do it, and they sent along Kaylum instead. It didn't go too well. Kaylum's gone off into the world, and I went off into the world, and that was that.

Kaylum didn't have much experience at that time. He was more of a cameraman than a director. It's one thing to have a camera and know how to use it, but I needed someone to do so much more. I had so many ideas. But I started to speak to Kaylum a bit, and I could see that he had the ability. It was the same sort of thing with TiiNY. They were both young, but they had potential. They were sharpening me up, but I made sure I was sharpening them up as well.

Flipz

Tobe came on board as his manager, then TiiNY became involved. There was a rave in Old Kent Road, and his DJ at the time couldn't come for whatever reason, and TiiNY was available. He just killed it. I remember he mixed an old-school grime instrumental with that Skepta track 'I Spy', and the place just exploded.

Kaylum

It was August 2013 when I first got to know Stormzy. I was fifteen. I didn't even have a camera at this stage. I was working for Pressplay Media. I'd always wanted to do a Stormzy video. I saw him one time at a Heavytrackerz event, behind the scenes, and said I wanted to make a video. So we made 'Straight Up'. And then I saw him again. This was when he was first coming up – 'Wicked Skengman 3' time. He was starting to do a lot of festivals, and I'd seen a video of him performing on Snapchat, and just thought: I have to document this. So I asked him if I could come and record a show, and he said, 'Yes, come to Reading and Leeds.' So I jumped on a train to Reading, and he just blew up. He shut it down. The tent was breaking. His performance was sick. I put it out on Link Up and people paid attention.

Akua

I had the most amazing boss and the most amazing mentor at Adidas, and the one thing I was taught when I first started was do what you say you're going to do. Get the job done. The only way to really build solid and long-lasting relationships is if people can trust you to get the job done. If they can trust you with their things, and know that you can make it happen, then that relationship is solid. They will come back to you every time. That trust is second to none.

So if I'm working with SB.TV, for example, and we say we're going to make 'This Is London', and we're going north, east, south and west, asking people to represent their ends, and bringing in Adidas and JD, and there will be billboards and bus advertising, and I pick up the phone and start talking to people, then they know that something is going to happen. I'm not going to just go quiet. I come good on what I say I'm going to do.

That's the problem. A lot of things are good ideas at the time. You don't necessarily know what's going to work and what isn't. You just have to be honest.

I just want to do good work. And just having the belief and passion and desire to do it as well as you can do, then that also builds up trust too.

I'm sometimes asked for careers advice, and I always say, 'Well, what do you enjoy doing?' Find the thing you enjoy doing and find a way to turn it into a job. Go and do some research and find out who gets paid to do these things. Take whatever that passion is, and find a way to get paid for it. And that's the only way you'll find a job you'll love.

If you ever get to a place where you're just doing things because you know that you can do them, then you're not growing as a person. You've got to be tenacious, and you've got to be ambitious, and you have to want to keep achieving and building momentum, and not be complacent. You can be happy with the work you've done, but there's always room for improvement. The process could be better. You can't just be producing the same thing again and again because you'll just get stuck. It's not healthy. Otherwise you could be doing anything. You might as well just go and get a job anywhere. If it's just repetition you might as well be standing on a shop floor. If you are trying to be creative and trying to push the boundaries in any way then you have to constantly grow and evolve.

work

Yeah I've got so much to prove and there's so much to do
But I know where I started
And I know where I'm heading, yeah, look, I've got
nothing to lose
And I'm still out here grafting
My sis taught me a lesson, I told her I owe it to you cause
Boy, this shit's been a struggle ever since we were kids
Coming home late, not even a penny to my name
Wouldn't even bother looking in the fridge
I ain't ever been the kind of guy to complain
You don't even ever hear me rapping about pain
Yeah man we've all got demons
So I can't hold feelings, I just knuckle up and then I pray
Just imagine if I didn't buss that case
Just imagine if I caught bus that day
Mum's life, I was in a rush that day
Swear man I'll never lose trust and faith
So sorry if I come across angry
If I love you there's no need to thank me
I'm just trying to be all that I can be
I just hope I bring it home for the family.

'Intro', *Dreamer's Disease*

introduction

Jude

In Part 2 the work begins. A team is formed, and paths connect. The question is, should you work to be a part of something, or work to create something new?

For many people, Stormzy's name appeared as if from nowhere. In the spring of 2015, after Stormzy appeared onstage with Kanye West at the Brit Awards, someone called him a 'back-up dancer' on Twitter. He recorded a freestyle in response: a vicious take-down of naysayers and all those wishing him ill, and a spectacular show of his verbal skill and confidence. Through his bars, Stormzy told everyone to shut up and listen. And they did. The freestyle, recorded in a park in south London on a hand-held camera, with Stormzy in a red tracksuit surrounded by his friends, immediately did numbers. It notched up 100,000 views on YouTube within weeks. People shared and debated it loudly on social media. Veterans in the game either loved it or hated it. Crowds went mad when it was performed, elderly buskers sang it on high streets, and a huge number of questionable YouTube covers proliferated. On 12 December 2015, Stormzy recited 'Shut Up' before Anthony Joshua's fight against Dillian Whyte for the British heavyweight title. It marked a new moment in history, projecting black excellence at its optimum: a home-grown boxer taking the world by storm, and a home-grown artist shutting down the O2 Arena with captivating energy. For a while, 'Shut Up' looked like it might even be in the running for the Christmas number one. It eventually reached number eight, several months after its initial release. At the time of writing, the song has sold over a million copies worldwide, and the original video has been viewed on YouTube over 80 million times, with nearly 500,000 likes. As Stormzy says in 'Cold', 'I just went to the park with my friends and I charted.'

He made it look easy. But there was a lot of work that led up to that moment. In 2013 and 2014, Stormzy's name had started to appear more regularly on social media. In March 2013 he released the 168 mixtape, recorded on a week's break from his engineering apprenticeship. In November 2013 he posted the first 'Wicked Skengman' freestyle on YouTube. The second appeared in February 2014, with his friend Flipz making an appearance. 'Don't even tark too much,' Stormzy says in the intro, introducing the now-iconic phrase to his growing audience. In May, 'Wicked Skengman 3' was posted, quickly followed by something more substantial: the *Dreamer's Disease* EP. Like 168, it was a bold, brash and brutally honest work, mixing the bravado of grime classics like 'Not That Deep' with soul-searching sections interrogating his life and the lessons he lived by:

> Quit my job, mum bugged out, made my choice,
> this is my life
> And I swear down I can't do this alone, may the
> good Lord be my guide.

By the end of the year, Stormzy had won Best Grime Act at the MOBOs, and was the first unsigned rapper ever to appear on *Later . . . With Jools Holland*.

Then in February 2015, Kanye West invited a host of grime stars to join him in a performance of 'All Day' at the Brit Awards. The rest, as they say, is history.

From the beginning, it was clear that Stormzy's career was not going to follow a traditional route. Despite gaining a level of attention and fame at a very early stage, Stormzy wasn't swayed by the allure of major labels, instead relying on himself, and those gathered around him, to take him to where he needed to go. The team would become increasingly important as Stormzy's success continued, allowing him the space to concentrate on his music, and to set into motion some of the events and moments that have made him who he is: the freestyle videos, the Adidas trainers giveaway, the birthday party at Thorpe Park, the festivals, the shows. Also granting him the necessary insights into the industry that would allow him to thrive outside of it. The #Merky DNA was expanded to include a level of benevolence and support not seen within the industry. As Stormzy went from strength to strength, so did the team.

The paths had converged and were leading upwards. Part 2 is about the work that was needed to progress.

4.

Tobe

I could see immediately what we could do. I can make sure
your music is on iTunes as well as other platforms. I can make
you a website. I can take care of your emails. I can write letters
for you. I can clean everything up.

I went through my contacts the night he asked me,
and pulled out anyone with any connection to the music
world at all. The next day I started calling them, to see what
advice they could give. Did anyone know any good lawyers, or
what studios we could use, or how to find live bands?

I had no musical background whatsoever, but I was learning
quickly. Every single day I felt like I was accomplishing
something. I was learning something from scratch and finding
a lot out. But it was something I wanted to learn. There's a bit
of a nerd in me as well. It was a quick transition.

As soon as I said I would do it, Stormzy ignited. He said
to me recently that the fact that I had given up my job meant
a lot to him. It meant it couldn't fail. He started making new

music and meeting new people and collaborating with other artists and picking up the pace, so I had to try and keep up. For a while I worried that I couldn't. I thought I might have to find an established manager, or bring in someone to help. I was still working out my notice at Land Rover.

People were worried for me. At the time, it was seen as if I was throwing my career away. I was wearing a suit to work every day. People used to say, 'What are you doing? Don't mess this up. I thought you were intelligent, Tobe?' But it became my fuel. It spurred me on. Not to prove anyone wrong, but just to show people that I knew myself. I never thought it was going to be as successful as it's become, but I knew I wouldn't regret the decision.

Even when I doubted myself, or felt like I was in over my head, I never thought I would go back. It was more: Am I going to have to bring someone in above me? Every time I spoke to Stormzy about it, if I floated an idea – 'Oh, I've met this person, and I think we could really work with them' – he'd just say, 'Fuck no. I can't work with that person.' Not because he didn't like them, but more just the fact that he has confidence in me.

It's like, even the small things. So, I didn't realise that you need to have a registered agent to get booked by some festivals. And that threw me off, straight away. I was like: OK, how do I do that? I didn't know any lawyers or accountants, I didn't know how to work with them, I had no clue. How do we set up something that has real credibility? I'm too small.

I've made hundreds of mistakes, but I learn from them. Next time, I know what to do. Working for someone else, and building their company for them, doesn't offer quite the same thing.

Kaylum

I started to roll with Stormzy a bit more. I think he liked the fact that I was hungry, and that I could do things quickly.

The next step was around the promotion of 'Wicked Skengman 4', I think. He was driving around giving people Adidas trainers, and I was just rolling with him, documenting it. I was like, 'Yo, you need to put all this shit out. This is sick content.' We were driving around London for a whole day.

Then we took his fans to Nando's, with *Noisey*. Then we shot 'Standard'. Bear in mind that I didn't own a camera. I had never owned a camera in my life at this point. I was just using Link Up TV's gear. So we shot this video, then we planned to drop a trailer. Link Up were like, 'Wait, where's it going?' and I said, 'Oh, on Stormzy's channel.' They said, 'No, that can't happen. Not if you're using our gear.'

That was when I broke. I wasn't being paid very much at all, and it just didn't make sense to me. I had been running around making videos for a long time by this point. I'd worked with Section Boyz and Yungen, and made them put stuff on their channels. I'd basically ditched my school life to better their channel. Then I clocked. I was like: Why don't I just do this myself? I just said, 'It's cool. Take back your stuff.' I was camera-less for a bit. Then Stormzy bought me a camera. Or actually, he gave me enough money to buy a camera and a laptop and stuff. A lot of money.

Austin

There's a correlation between having star quality and doing the basics correctly, time after time after time after time. And during those early days, Stormzy did all the basics. He turned up on time, he was polite, he wasn't afraid to ask questions, and he listened to the answers. All big stars do the same.

We had a bit of an exploratory meeting at first. We were just saying, well, this is what we do at 1Xtra, this is how we want to support you, send us your music and let's stay in touch. So we did. Eventually he recorded the *Dreamer's Disease* EP, and 'That's Not Deep', and we put it out and supported it. People support him now, but at the time, people were saying, 'It's all an industry hype. The public aren't into him.' But we knew they were. Industry people are paid to make bets. And some industry people could see that he was a Messi, he was a Usain Bolt. This was someone who was going to make history. But because the industry were doing that, it was conflated with fake hype. But it wasn't. It was a realness. And we were right. He went from 800 followers to 8,000 followers to 80,000 followers to 800,000 followers very quickly.

Alec (Twin)

We were working with Jacob Banks on a track called 'Move With You' at the time, and we'd just put together this remix with Wretch and I thought that Stormzy should also get involved. My thinking was: If he can keep up with Wretch on this record, then he's a G. And he did. I spoke to Wretch after, and he was like, 'This guy is the guy.' Stormzy took it seriously. He was on time, he did everything properly. And as always with Stormz, the verse was sick!

His real passion, interest and knowledge of music was incredible. He was a real fan of music, and a fan of music being done well. He used to call me up and say, 'Bruv, bruv, have you heard the new Meghan Trainor record? Perfectly executed pop song. Do you know why? . . .' I loved that.

Tobe

When I first started working with Stormzy, I used to wear a shirt and shoes to meetings. And then I thought to myself one day: I'm not comfortable. This isn't what I'd choose to wear. I work with my friends. It's a beautiful thing. I really don't have to impress that side of the table any more. It's the other way around. *You* have to impress *me*. Either I like what you're saying and we can work together, or I don't and we go elsewhere.

That frustration is real. I've actually sat down with people who can't understand it. They can't comprehend that people are recording music, putting albums together and getting into the charts by themselves.

How I started out, I realised straight away, if I presented myself as Stormzy's manager, his friend who grew up with him, I might get dismissed: 'Oh, he's picked the wrong person.' People would deal with me because Stormzy'd put me in front of them, but I'd just be a pawn. So what I decided to do was make sure it was very difficult to tell. Not because I'm not proud to be a young black guy who's helped his good friend get to a place we couldn't have imagined. My email is anonymous. I'd sign my email in a way that made me anonymous. I'd throw you off, so the first meeting with me is the first time you'll know who I am: 'Wait, I didn't expect you to look like this.'

When I'm out and about with Stormzy, I'll be dismissed: 'It's just one of Stormzy's friends.' And he'll be like, 'No, he's my manager.' And you can see the look in people's eyes. We're in a position now where I don't get the questioning look, but it's more of a 'Wow, he's capable of producing all of this, managing this career.' It's not necessarily a positive step – not positive for young black people in general – but it's positive in terms of you can't question where it's come from, because you appreciate the result.

Rachel

A year or so in, my friend said to me, 'Why don't you just set up something on your own?' I thought it was a bit premature. I had little experience, I'd never even run an album campaign before and had no clue as to what something like that might involve. But he said to me, 'So what – you can learn. Don't take on loads of people, just focus on one or two people at a time who you're passionate about.' I thought about it for a while, and decided to go for it.

The name 'Wired' came from a very brief brainstorm at my friend's house. They were playing PlayStation whilst we were discussing possible names, and as simplistic as it may sound – it

Tour life, Europe
and America.

First MOBO.

Ghana trip with Twin B.

'Know Me From' video,
February 2015.

The Brit Awards and Red Bull Culture Clash, 2015.

'Shut Up' video, May 2015.

'All these sleepless nights and these cheap-arse flights.' 'Dreamer's Disease'.

AJ.

BBC 1Xtra Live, Leeds.

Jet life.

'I might sing but I ain't sold out. Nowadays all of my shows sold out.' 'Shut Up'.

Rachel.

TiiNY.

'Man just talk, don't talk, be steady.' 'Wicked Skengman

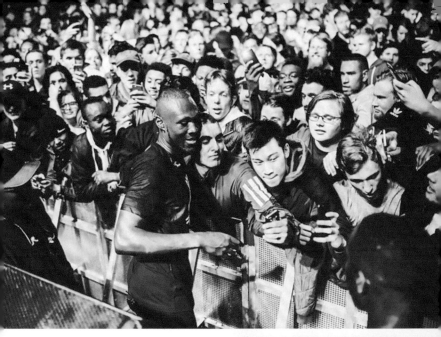

Europe, London, V Festival, 2016.

was. There were wires everywhere in the lounge. And that was it – Wired PR. I bought the website domain, set up a Twitter and email account, and just went from there.

A month or so later, a journalist I'd liaised with previously – Joss – got in touch and said she thought the new company sounded exciting, and asked if I was looking for any help. So we met up, chatted, and she came on board. It's been us two ever since, and she's now not only my business partner but also one of my closest friends.

The early days were fairly tough; however, I suspect 90 per cent of start-ups endure a hard first few years. Filling in our first tax return was the easiest thing in the world, because we'd made so little money. It was fairly stressful at points: there were bills to pay with limited money coming in and a lot of work to do. However, there's a different level of commitment when it's your own project, and we were both so hungry to make it work we knew we just had to get on with it.

Tobe

When we first got involved in music, we realised that whatever we put out has to be truthful.

We didn't want to shake off the grime tag, because it was important to us. Stormzy is a child of grime, and some of his favourite artists are grime artists. He is a grime kid. But grime can mean different things. He was making the 'Wicked Skengman' freestyles, but he was also making freestyles that were more pure rap. He was also listening to Whitney Houston. He was making Justin Bieber covers. He has range.

Grime is a genre, but it's also a culture. You can still be a grime kid and not only make grime.

Stormzy has this good point about grime. You might be a grime purist, but almost every artist you like without exception has tried something different at some point.

Alec (Twin)

I put Tobe and Stormz in contact with Rachel, who I'd been working with for a bit and knew. A lot of press requests were coming in, and he needed someone to communicate on his behalf. Someone who's just a bit different to them. From having conversations with the managers, I realised they were just looking at this six-foot-five black guy, with a lot of freestyles online, and not seeing anything else. They didn't get it. They weren't seeing the pop potential. They didn't see his artistry. But I thought how the world sees him needed a bit of thought. Rachel is passionate and loves great music. She saw it all straight away.

It took a sec for them to connect. She is amazing. They then met Kieran, his lawyer. Kieran is a G. And his live agent, Craig. Great people I know well. Stormz and Tobe were forming a great team.

Rachel

I first heard of Stormzy through the 'Wicked Skengman' freestyles. I remember watching 'Wicked Skengman 3', and just thinking it was one of the best freestyles I'd seen from a rapper in a very long time. I then went on to scour his YouTube channel and just sat there watching all the videos he'd ever put out. I was in complete awe of this kid's talent. I sent him a tweet, asking if he had a manager I could reach out to, but he never replied. I remember he only had around 12,000 followers at this point, so I knew he'd seen it, ha! Shortly after I reached out on Twitter, he released his *Dreamer's Disease* EP – and I tweeted him again. No reply. So I was like: OK, maybe he doesn't know what PR is. He's probably just thinking: Who's this girl? Leave me alone!

And then one night in early February 2015, I was with a friend in east London when I got a call from Twin B. He said, 'Rach, I'm with Stormzy and Tobe now, and they need a PR. They've got loads of requests coming in . . .' and just reeled off a list of publications. 'Can you speak to Tobe?' So he looped us in on email. I will forever be in Twin's debt for that connect. Tobe and I then met in a random pub near Clapham North. I explained what I did and what my vision was for Stormzy and his PR. Tobe then talked about their vision. I'd never heard a manager speak about their artist in the way that Tobe did that day – it was inspiring. But then I soon learned that Tobe will always inspire me – he's a remarkable manager.

Stormzy

The only time there was doubt was with the first addition to our team, who was Rachel. Me and Tobe had been mashing it up, and we'd won our first MOBO, and it was like us two against the world. We were doing shows everywhere, and we didn't even have a booking agent. Then one day Tobe said,

'Listen, we need to get a PR.' I was like, 'Wait, what the fuck is a PR?' Tobe explained it to me, and I wasn't convinced. I was like, 'What are they going to do? Get me photoshoots?' Tobe said, 'Listen, it's going to cost, as well.'

This was at a time when we were skint. But the other thing we've always agreed on is the need to invest in what we're doing. Whether it's £100,000 or £1, it doesn't matter. If it's helping us move forward, then we do it. But at that time, we had no money. Any money we were making was going straight back in. I said, 'Bruv! That's nuts.' But he told me that we had to do it. And I trust him. We're on the same wavelength, most of the time. There have only been a couple of things that we haven't agreed on, and Rachel was one of them. But I trusted him. I said yes.

Rachel started coming round, and I was doing photoshoots and things like that, and I still wasn't sure. But very quickly I realised what PR was, and also that we had the best fucking publicist in the whole game. It's more astonishing that she was kind of at the start of her career, too.

The same thing happened with Trev. And Kieran, my lawyer. And my booking agent. I just had to trust Tobe. He knew exactly what he was doing.

The only time I'd really taken the lead was with Akua, AK. I have never told her this, but I knew, even when I first met her, that she would come and work with us. We've always been close. I've always had mad love for her, and seen her as a bit of a big sister. But at that time there was nothing to suggest that she would come and work with us. It was a bit audacious. She's a big don in this ting. She doesn't need to come over to this start-up, #Merky.

Tobe

The first person to join the team after me was Rachel.

My management style is largely dictated by how I think. So if I see a new artist I like, I try to find out as much about them as possible. And that information almost always exists somewhere online. So immediately after I started working with Stormzy, I thought: Well, we're going to need to put some information together. Just a fact sheet. There was very little available online, beyond what he was saying on social media.

I was also reaching out to a lot of publications at the time, to see if we could get a bit more exposure. Do a profile on him and let people know he's here. But I was always getting the same response: 'OK, he sounds interesting, put me in touch with his PR.' I was like: Hang on a second, what's a PR?

When she told me how she saw Stormzy, and what she thought he'd done right, and what he could improve, I was very impressed. She was lovely, but she was also honest. She wasn't afraid to share her opinions. I met with three other people just to be sure. They were all full of praise, but had nothing constructive to say. Honesty was so important. Like Akua – she was offering advice because she wanted us to win.

Kaylum

Some channels are just about the money. But not all of them. GRM, for example. They're a lot more welcoming to directors and to artists. They even chip in at times for artists I shoot.

Then it was the Stormzy one-take video in Tokyo. Me,

Akua, Tobe and Stormzy went to Japan. The second we landed we had a meeting, then we just wandered around looking for nightspots. I had one camera with me, but no lighting, no nothing. It was an important moment for grime. People were following us around. I was documenting it all on Snapchat; we finished the video and edited it in two hours. It really only worked out because of the way that Stormzy is, and how he can perform. From that point on I had a bit of a name for myself.

I still really had nothing. No lighting, no gimbal, no nothing. But everything started to happen. It was fun, but I wanted to do more. I was determined to improve. And being around Stormzy helped. He was always pushing me to level up. At that time I had about ten videos up on Instagram, and I'd made about a thousand. If I didn't think it was amazing, I wouldn't even put my name on it sometimes. I was just trying to be the best I could be. That's just how he is. If you're not above him, or at least on the same wavelength as him, then it won't work.

Akua

When I left Adidas I just wanted to work in football. I had finished my master's, I felt equipped, I had my few contacts, I had my Adidas background. But just before I left, one of the last things I did was this Tokyo trip with Stormzy. We'd never been to Tokyo before, and we had a lot of downtime, and did plenty of talking. I spent a good deal of time with the guys, and I remember just thinking: I love being around you lot. We'd come so far so quickly. I mean, when I first met him he didn't have a manager. And me and Tobe had a really great relationship. And I still wanted to help them. I felt that when I left, I might still be able to help. I could still provide input in some way.

After Adidas I did think I still wanted to be a part of Stormzy's journey. They felt like family. And I was so nervous to ask. When I left, I remember being so nervous asking, 'Do you want me to be part of the team?' It was strange. I mean, I've always been Akua Adidas, that's how people have me saved in their phones, that's how I'm introduced. I'm still asked questions about Adidas today. But Tobe said, 'Well, can you start now?' And that for me was all I needed to hear. I just wanted to be a part of it, and they said yes.

Tobe

Something I notice when I listen back to Stormzy is that he always supports people from south. Take the song he made with Chip, 'Hear Dis'. Stormzy's talking about Mark and Danny, his friends from Croydon. He's proud of them. He's always been quick to represent his people. We came into this understanding that point. Stormzy's whole thing has always been: It needs to be multiplied. It can't just be his journey.

Alec (Twin)

The funny thing is I met Ed Sheeran really early on, as well, back when he was sofa-surfing. I think he might have even slept on my couch a couple of times. Him and Stormzy are the same human being. They're both ambitious, they're both very intelligent, they're both ridiculously talented and they're both really nice people. And they're similar in terms of what they take in, what they observe and recognise and take forward into their own work.

As soon as I started speaking to Stormzy I told Ed about him and I think it's one of the only times I had ever done that with Ed. I said, 'Right, I've just met someone you need to connect with. This is the guy. Trust me when I say he's more than an MC. This guy could be an incredible artist.' Ed had just set up a label here, and thought, 'Oh, maybe he's someone we could work with.' I said, 'Maybe, but you just need to meet him. I think he needs a bit of help and guidance, maybe.'

We spent a bit of time going back and forth about setting up a meeting, and then Ed said, 'Why don't you come up here?' So I called Stormzy. 'Can you come meet me up west with Tobe?' They drove in and I said, 'Listen, we're going up to see Ed in Suffolk.' It was mad. We got near Ed's house and called him up to get directions. He said, 'Just find this pub and wait in the car park and I'll come and find you.' Stormzy had just bought this brand-new Audi, so we're sitting there in the car park waiting when an old 2004 Mini trundles in and parks alongside it. The window rolls down and it's Ed. 'What's happening? Follow me.' Stormzy looks at me and says, 'I've got this all wrong, haven't I.'

It was wicked day. We get into his house and Ed's talking about a song he's just sold to Justin Bieber. He said, 'I don't have a recording of it, but I'll play it to you.' It was 'Love Yourself'. Six months later when it came out, Stormzy called me and said, 'Bruv! That's that tune, isn't it?' And it's a bad boy.

They hit it off immediately. They really got on. But I felt like they were kindred spirits as artists as well. I think maybe Stormzy really needed to speak to someone like Ed at that stage. There were things that Ed had gone through that I thought Stormzy needed to know about, and things that I thought he could learn, in terms of what is really possible, and the right way to go about achieving and handling success, and vice versa. Ed also asked Stormz a million questions. This was before ×, when Ed really became one of the biggest male artists in the world, but he was still pretty big. And he was grounded, and nice, and knew how to work.

Flipz

He's worked very hard for what he's got.

First of all it was people from round our ends. Grime fans. It started to change with 'Know Me From'. Whenever Stormzy played that, it went nuts. The moshpit crew. There aren't many tracks that get that kind of a reaction, every time. It was the same response wherever we went. That was when I realised things were taking off. We'd do shows in Birmingham, or up north, and everyone was just going wild. It was crazy.

DJ TiiNY

It's not about the money or the fame or the girls at all. This is what I'm trying to tell my girl! It's not about that at all. Tobe used to point me in particular directions. We'd look at what Wiz Khalifa was doing on tour, what Tinie Tempah was doing, and he said, 'Just watch this and we'll see how things go.' He was just giving me a heads-up at what we could get into. Learning where DJs got their music from and that sort of thing.

At this time I was speaking to Stormzy, but also balancing college, working in Gap in Kingston, and DJing. I was working in the shop one day and Stormzy shouted me saying, 'Lethal Bizzle's got me on his tour. Do you want to come and do it?' I said, 'Oh, I can't. I've got work.' I thought that if I worked hard enough, I could get the same kind of money from DJing. But then I said to myself: Wait, donny's going with Bizzle! This is an opportunity that he's giving to me! So I bought a train ticket to Manchester, went up for the show, missed three days of work. They were calling me, but I just ignored it. And when I came back they didn't say anything.

People thought that I was big. I was getting tracks to play and that from boys that made music in my year, but they didn't realise I was in the same position as them. I was still trying to come up.

There was a difference with Stormzy. Stormzy was pushing. His thing has always been if you put in work, you'll get far. He was doing his ting, so if I wanted to be in his circle, I had to do my ting too. So I just thought: Well, let me work hard. I might be wavy, but people have got to hear me. So I worked hard. I got guest mixes with a lot of people: MistaJam, DJ Target, Charlie Sloth, BBC Asian Network, Kiss, Capital, 1Xtra, Triple J Radio in Australia. I worked with everyone I wanted to.

We had the dreams, of course, like all young boys do, but then it was the work that got us there. Soon I was heading off overseas with Tobe and Stormzy. It's happened fast, but it wasn't like we didn't expect it.

Kaylum

I was always welcomed. I knew Flipz, I think I knew TiiNY before I joined the team, but when I first started to be involved, everyone was welcoming. Everyone. They realised that I just wanted to work. To be honest, if I asked for anything, it would get sorted. Akua helps. Rachel helps – she's even given me work outside of the team. They've always wanted what's best for me. It's really more like a family than a team. Tobe always used to say, 'You're you as well. You should have your own thing built as well.' It's the best of both.

Stormzy

If I'm being honest, man don't work with clowns. My clown threshold is very low. You don't have to be perfect, because that's impossible. But there are different types of perfect.

It's like Moussa Dembélé: perfect player. He doesn't get the praise, but if I was a football manager, he'd be in my team. You know why? He's going to win the ball and pass it. He's not going to try and run down the wing. He's not going to fuck up. He's going to do his job, and do it well.

People overcomplicate things. Some musicians have come to me and say, 'Oh, man needs a manager. Man needs a radio plugger. Man needs press shots. What should I do?' And I always say, 'Bro, you're a musician. Make music. That's your one job. Don't overcomplicate it.'

I've only been in the game for four years, and in that time, everything has changed. When I first started, I never would have thought of asking older musicians questions like that. Something has changed. Maybe it's social media. That's the only reason I can think of. Because for a younger generation, a profile is everything. But it's not. What I'm saying isn't some secret key to life. It's like, if you're a footballer, score goals. If you're a musician, make music. Get in the studio. That's your bread and butter. There's no secret to it.

5.

Tobe

We had released 'Shut Up' in summer 2015, and it had barely scratched the chart. It was only when we performed with Anthony Joshua before the Dillian Whyte fight in December that things started to change. Performing just before the fight meant that so many people were force-fed the music. There was an audience there that would never have listened to Stormzy's music, who would never have given him a chance. And 'Shut Up' was just perfect. It's essentially saying shut up to the naysayers, or to anyone who's trying to hold you back. It's a song of defiance. Everyone's wanted to tell someone to shut up at some point in their lives.

Immediately after the performance we had all sorts of people coming up to us saying congratulations. And then a couple of days later, at the airport, the same thing happened again. Older men, dads, families. All sorts. When you can find a way to reach these people you can really grow.

Trevor

I'm quite protective of my name, and of my brand. I didn't really want to bring people in to help, because I thought I had to do it all myself. I kept it small. I need to know absolutely everything. Attention to detail is so important. But there came a point where I just couldn't do it all any more. I was turning a lot of people down simply because I hadn't put a proper team together.

Then in the summer of 2015 I was at a festival in Bath with Wretch, hanging around backstage, when this guy came up to me and said, 'Are you Trevor Williams? My name's Tobe, and I'm working with Stormzy.' He said that a few people had mentioned my name to him so he thought he'd come over and say hi. So I said hi. He seemed like a nice guy, but I didn't really think anything of it.

And then a little while later Tobe hit me up and asked if I wanted to come along to their London show, at KOKO. The problem is, I can't just watch a show. I'm looking at everything, seeing what's working, what isn't. The show was good, but there were aspects that I felt didn't work or weren't needed. To be fair, that was the accepted standard for grime shows in the industry at the time.

One of the things I most like and respect about Tobe is that if he doesn't know something he'll ask. And I don't think he knew a lot about production. A couple of weeks later he called me again and said, 'Trevor, we need your help.' Stormzy had two shows in one night: one in Skegness and one in Birmingham, and they had to work out a way to get him across in time. I said, 'OK, I think I should be able to put one of my drivers on it.' And I was at the show in Skegness anyway, so I could help out there. I knew some of the team already.

It was quite funny. When I met Stormzy in Skegness, he kept it quite close. I walked into his dressing room and said, 'Hi Stormzy, I'm Trev. Just wanted to let you know that your driver's here.' He was just like, 'Cool.' So I asked, 'You good? Is there anything you need?' 'No, I'm good.' As if to say, 'Who's this guy?' LOL!

But I left it at that. I didn't think he liked touring. In his head, touring was headaches and drama.

Flipz

As the shows got bigger, TiiNY needed to be more a part of it. He couldn't just be the DJ any more. Then Trev came along, and organised everything. Before that it was Tobe. On top of everything else he was doing, he was speaking to the venues, booking cars and accommodation, everything. You don't realise how much there is to do. Because we have such a hectic schedule, and because we're so busy, we don't really have time to waste. It's not good if we land somewhere and have to wait half an hour for a car. Trevor took care of all that – so Stormzy could relax, and concentrate on his performance, and on the music.

As he's got bigger, the level of professionalism has increased. Our slickness has increased. It all rises at one level. And it's always rising.

Ayesha

I been friends with Akua for years – I am close with her cousin and when we met we just clicked. At the time, I was studying Anthropology and wanted to work for the United Nations. However, as time went on I realised my passion for football could turn into a career, and started working within the industry. Akua, our friend Whitney and I come as a three, so whenever Akua would be at festivals, concerts, events and so on, Whitney and I would be there, and vice versa.

From there I got to know Mike, Tobe and all the boys. Around the time of Mike's Leicester concert, I was in the process of leaving my job – that night I remember having a general conversation with Tobe about all the things he had constantly going on. A couple of weeks later, I received a text from Akua asking if Tobe could have a meeting with me.

Akua has always had mass amounts of potential. She is always doing more than what is required of her, constantly pushing the boundaries of the expectation she has of herself and the people she is working with. Which is why her and Mike are a match made in heaven: they are both visionaries, one just has a concept and the other has the execution. It's the marrying of ambitions. Before I joined the team, I thought you needed the support of a record label, a big branding company and a powerhouse PR company to execute to the extent the #Merky team was. It was a massive revelation that, in fact, it is their independence that makes all they do possible. Stormzy's talents do not just lie in music – if they did, things wouldn't work the way they do. It's not just a strive for greatness, it's the uncomfortableness of doing anything other than great work, music related or not. Everything he and the team do is iconic.

Tobe

As soon as I met Akua, I kind of felt that she was bigger than a single brand. When you work for a business, you do what you need to do in terms of your job role, but she always went above and beyond. She wasn't just serving Adidas. She understood where we were coming from. That passion belongs somewhere else. I'd mentioned the idea of her working with us in a tentative way, but never believed that she would want to do it. I just thought that we'd need to be a lot bigger, like a major corporation, before she would consider it. And she's completely changed the way we work. There's nothing she can't do.

I was doing so much. And for a while I was even his unofficial tour manager, until we brought Trevor in.

Ayesha, too. She came in as my assistant, but she's the team executive. She's going to be CEO one day.

It's a small team, but it's a team made of bosses. Trevor has his own company. Akua has her own company. Rachel has her own company.

I say to Stormzy: 'Brother, do you realise how good we are?'

Stormzy

It all evolved quite naturally. At first I was doing everything myself, or with Flipz and a few of the mandem, and then Tobe came on board. Then I needed a DJ, so TiiNY came on board. Then festivals wouldn't book us unless we had an agent. Up until then, I'd been booking everything myself. So we got a booking agent. Then Tobe said we needed a PR, so Rachel came on board. Then the shows started to get bigger, so we got a tour manager. And so on.

Infrastructure is a word I always use. This is where the team comes in. I might have an idea, but the team see everything that needs to happen and that needs to be put into place for that idea to happen.

It's a difficult thing, because life gets in the way. I can't do it myself. I can't afford to. The ideas I have, the music I want to make, the shows I want to do, the companies I want to build, the ideas I want to execute, are too big for me to do on my own. But I can have an idea, and think about it, and do a bit of research, and hand it over to one of the team. And I know that I can leave it, and by the time I come back, it will be ready to go.

Maybe I do a little bit more work now, because the ideas are a bit bigger, but it's the team that makes them happen. They're creating while I'm doing what I've got to do. You can't half-step it.

Rachel

Working with Stormzy wasn't like working with anyone else. The first week I came on board, he didn't actually have a phone. He'd just call from various numbers with ideas of how we could garner support on his latest release, 'Know Me From', which had recently come out. It was steadily climbing the charts and was close to breaking the Top 40 – and this was rare. It had been years since an underground track had broken through in the charts, let alone a track from a fairly unknown artist.

I soon realised he was extremely impulsive – in the best form – and so I knew that I had to do things differently with him. I remember thinking we needed some kind of viral element to the 'Know Me From' campaign, so I called up Hoff, Head of Video at Noisey, and explained an idea where we'd come down to the Noisey HQ, Stormzy would perform 'Know Me From' via a live stream and a load of fans would turn up. I remember Stormz actually leaked the news on his Twitter earlier than he should have and the guys over at Noisey were a little concerned we'd have a hundreds of fans turn up. That we did, although it was manageable and an incredible atmosphere. The event was a success with thousands of people also tuning in to the live stream. For me that was the foresight our PR strategy – unconventional thinking.

I remember everything was snowballing and soon enough Stormzy was performing 'Shut Up' at the O2 Arena for Anthony Joshua's ring walk. That was December 2015. The next evening, the track was sitting in the iTunes chart at maybe, forty – which was flippin' impressive. Stormzy called me and said, 'Rach, I want to go for the Christmas number one spot.' I knew how competitive it was at that time of the year – we would also be challenging the infamous X Factor single – but I thought, let's do it, the hashtag was soon trending online and the promotional campaign began. Before we knew it, we were at 10/1 odds with Coral and finished the week at number eight, even beating the X Factor winner's single. I remember saying to the team, 'This is nuts.'

I don't know when it transpired that I became a part of the #Merky team, I just know that soon enough we all genuinely cared for one another. We didn't have the backing of a major label. We just had the team and often there were times we were doing stuff that wasn't really within the remit of our particular roles, but it's just what we had to do. Sometimes when you're in an industry that's so fast-paced, it's hard to see exactly what it is that you're doing and to acknowledge the journey that you're on – you just get on with it.

DJ TiiNY

As I grew up, in the back of my head I always knew I had to be serious in my role, too. I'd been through the ups and downs of being on stage with Stormzy, making mistakes and that, but I've learned to be focused and put my head down. Meeting Stormzy and everyone really motivated me and kept me on the ball. They're happy for me and they're proud, and I'm happy for them too.

It's all a big family. It's like, we've been to so many places together, had so many experiences together, and I've had so many good moments. Take the first time he won a MOBO. This is a boy who lived fifteen minutes away from me. He won that award and he blessed all of us.

Ayesha

Initially, I was meant to come in as Tobe's assistant. But I don't often deal with Tobe's personal stuff like an assistant would. My role mainly pertains to #Merky as a business, and being Tobe's right hand. As clichéd as it may sound, we are generally a family – you're part of a team where you are respected and valued, and that type of environment is going to be more conducive to your productivity. You want to do better and be better, not just for yourself but also for the people you care about.

Akua

It's a big family unit. And that's really important. We care about each other. It was the same sort of thing at Adidas. It was a family unit. Once you're in, you're in.

6.

Trevor

2016 was busy. 2016 was the foundation.

We started to work with Stormzy and the team a bit more on their UK tour, and by that stage I'd brought in my sidekick Bronski (Mr Creative Genius) and Raph aka 'Benitez' (a name given to him by Stormzy) to help build the live shows. He was headlining the Great Escape festival in Brighton, so I thought I'd go along too. That day was mad. It was the FA Cup Final, and we all went to Wembley to watch it, and then drove down to Brighton. It was a bit of a turning point. I was driving down in my car, so I went to get in, and Stormzy shouted out, 'Yo, I'll roll with Trev!' So we drove down together.

There was a lot that needed to change. Most of the places we were playing we just turned up. We had a little room backstage, and that was about it. We were just another artist. No one really knew who we were. I was trying to work out who we were, too.

These guys were mad. They didn't have a set list when we first started working together. TiiNY and Stormzy would just sit down ten minutes before a show and talk through it.

When we arrived at shows there were often like thirty men waiting there. I was like: Wait, we need to have a conversation about personnel. How many of these people actually need to be here? Stormzy is rolling deep!

But on the other side, he would do a lot on his own. He would turn up to airports without anyone. Sometimes it was just me. I had to say, 'Stormzy, you need to have a plan here. You need some security. I can't protect you on my own.' Sometimes he would even drive himself to the shows. He was headlining the 1Xtra stage at Reading Festival and he was saying to me that he's going to drive himself! I said, 'No, Stormz, it's no longer that. Stay where you are, I'm sending a driver. Don't be on that "I'll do it myself" shit. You need to prepare.'

Stormzy

By 2016, we basically had the team in place. It was a sick time, but I didn't really know what was going on. It wasn't like I knew that we were about to create *Gang Signs & Prayer*; we were just moving forward.

The more I think, the more I remember. It's been four years of madness. When I think about everything we've gone through, it's crazy. When we talk about it now, we can remember bits and pieces, but not everything. I was talking to Tobe and TiiNY the other day, laughing about the time we had a play-fight backstage at one of the shows. Me and Tobe against TiiNY and Kaylum. We were fucking them up! But we couldn't remember where it was.

It could have been Dublin, Australia, Denmark, anywhere in the world. Or there was a time when a firework went off at one of the shows and it almost hit me. Couldn't remember where it was. Or the time we were late for our plane, and had to run through the airport, with security chasing us. Or the time Fran, my agent, got dragged away by the police. He'd gone through customs at the airport and came back to say goodbye. And the police just said, 'Excuse me, you can't do that.' I couldn't tell you where that was. No idea. It's all become a blur.

Tobe

Stormzy has always been aware of perception, or how people will see him. How people will take him wanting more. We always knew that there's a truth in the world that isn't represented in the world. We have our own concerns. And we are worried about what's happening in the world around us. But it's how you act that's important.

Stormzy

There's a real problem with our culture in the way that artists are pigeonholed. I was determined it would never happen with me. I'd come out guns blazing. I'll go and spit in the park, then I'll go on *Live Lounge* and sing something.

I had a little trick. Whenever I'd go on *Live Lounge*, I always did a mad singing medley. My first one was tragic. My singing voice just wasn't there. Some people appreciated it, but even they were saying, 'I see what you tried to do there.' But you have to understand, I was setting myself up. It was me being fearless, and showing the world that I love R&B, I love singing, I love experimenting with music. That's the artist I am, that's my truth. This ain't new. Go back and listen to 168.

Ayesha

Tobe is one of the most dedicated and headstrong people I've ever met. The way his mind works is rare, it is instinct. It's that pure self-belief in himself and his team – as he always says, 'God's got us.' Tobe and Stormzy balance each other out – he is not just his manager, he is his friend and has been since they were kids, so they understand each other on a deeper level. Together they have navigated the industry without years of experience behind them, just a driven faith in each other.

Stormzy is super creative and innovative. You'll be around him, and he'll say, 'I don't want to follow what everyone else is doing, I want to do this.' It may the craziest leftfield idea, but it will make sense. And the team makes it happen. Tobe will have a plan, Akua will have a plan – everyone has that one vision in mind. Coming into the team was inspiring. It is not individuals operating for one fundamental cause, it is a collective: we all move as one, and get stuff done.

Akua

Everything we do comes from a simple idea. When you work for a brand, you can sit and come up with ideas all day long. But then you have several layers of approval or red tape to get through, and there are changes to make, and deadlines to meet, and stakeholders to please, and so by the time you get to the final product, if you even get to the final product, it's so stripped back or modified or limited that no one cares any more.

One of the big things I learned really quickly working with Stormzy was to change that perspective. Stormzy would text me in the middle of the night and say, 'AK, can we do this?' And I'd say, 'No, probably not.' And he'd say, 'Why not?' And I wouldn't have an answer. Only, well, it's too crazy, or too grand, or too different. And he'd say, 'But can we ask?' Eventually I discovered that he was right – the more you ask, the more yeses you get. It was a massive learning curve for me. So when he wanted to have a birthday party at Thorpe Park, at first I thought: No. But it happened. Now, no idea is too big, no idea is too crazy. And if we explore every option and it can't happen then it can't happen. But at least we've asked.

You can have these big ideas, but do you genuinely believe that they can happen? If so, then why not make them happen?

You can't be intimidated. You've got to remember that when you really break it down, the people you speak to are just doing a job. It's like Beyoncé at Coachella. When you first watch her performance, you think: Wow, that's the most incredible thing I've ever seen. Impossible to replicate. But if you break it down, it's just a lot of people working towards the same goal. The band, the tour manager, the set designer, the choreographer, the dancers, the lighting engineer, the technicians, Beyoncé – everyone is on the same page, working to produce the same thing. It's not quite as daunting.

And that's how we think. We see everything as possible.

Ayesha

When you've got an artist who's popular there will always be people who want you to go in another direction. The team acts as a filter for one another. There is so much stuff that comes to me that Tobe will never hear, and so much shit that Tobe hears that will never get to Stormzy. We will only say things if we know that they are worth his time. That only comes from knowledge and experience of one another. Stormzy won't know every technical detail. Say with his birthday party at Thorpe Park a couple years ago, he just turned up and had a great time. He was like, 'Akua how did you pull this together?' Even then I don't think he realised the extent of how much work had gone into it.

Stormzy

The way I work has changed over time. At the beginning, about four or five years ago, I was this mad, young, super-hungry, energetic artist. That was the energy I needed. I had to go to the studio, record a track, make a video, put it out. And do it again. But now, I have different aims. What I'm trying to do requires thought, and care. There's a different weight to what we're doing.

Everyone's showed me the ropes in their field. One thing I really enjoy doing is speaking to younger artists. Because I've just got a pool of knowledge to spill. I always say, 'This isn't me trying to be arrogant or patronising, I just know this is how it's supposed to go.' I've been lucky enough to work with some of the best in the business. 'No, you shouldn't be travelling like that.' 'No, your manager shouldn't be doing that.' 'No, that's not how PR works.'

It's like if Rio Ferdinand, at the height of his powers, moved to a dead team, he wouldn't be the same player. He's the best in part because he's surrounded by the best. He's used to having Scholes there.

And that's what I've learned. Trev telling me, 'No, you can't just turn up to a show fifteen minutes before. You've got to get there early, go through the set list, do your warm-up, have some water, get on.' Today I was at a publicity event, and it was a good one. I know that because Rachel has taught me what to expect.

You can only be great if you have great people around you. And I've got that. It goes back to the idea of excellence. We just have such high standards. Nothing gets past us. My job really is to ask questions, but it's got to the stage now where I don't really have to ask too many questions. I trust everyone. I never ask a question unless I think I have a right to.

When we first started, I asked a lot of questions: Why has it been edited like that? Why are we speaking to these people? Why can I not hear my voice at a show? Is it because the mic levels weren't right? Is it because the festival's speakers weren't very good? Is it a problem with the sound more generally? Is it the engineer's fault? What happened? And why?

Because we need to make sure it never happens again.

We haven't achieved all the things we want to achieve. This is just the start. We're just building the foundations.

It's not like I want to be someone. It's almost disrespectful to think that I could be a Jay-Z. It's ignoring all the work and effort and thought that he has put into getting to where he is. Me saying I want to be the next Jay-Z suggests that I'm just going to waltz into it. I recognise what needs to be done. Excellence is the key word. It's always been my mantra. If you're striving for excellence, you know you can't fail.

It's something I've always done naturally. Not that I've always been excellent, but that I wanted everything I did to be excellent. My mum drilled it into me. And then Twin drilled it into me. When I play you a tune, I don't want you to think it's good, I want it to be excellent.

Trevor

I never really had a mentor, or anyone who showed me a way forward in the industry. It's one of the reasons we want to give back. The figures I looked up to when I was growing up were all American.

At the same time, you often know what you want to do without someone trying to shove it down your throat. I think that's what we had.

Tobe

In the beginning, social media was a blessing. We were working on a shoestring, and it was free and it was easy. You get instant reactions. You can notify people about new music. We couldn't afford billboards, or a big marketing campaign, so social media was really our only outlet. It was our main resource for a long time.

Ayesha

Stormzy is nerdy. He's a bookworm. He loves Connect 4.
He's got a poker table, he's got all kinds of board games. He
has games nights with Maya and his friends. He's even got a
whiteboard where he keeps scores. The other day I was at his
house with Trevor and Akua getting ready to leave when Trev
spotted Connect 4, and of course he had to challenge Stormz.
We then had to wait another hour while the two of them went
back and forth playing.

DJ TiiNY

From my eighteenth birthday or so I was spending most of my
time abroad. In fact, I think I've had all of my last birthdays
abroad. We've travelled around the world. Touring gave me a
big boost.

The chemistry that me and Stormzy bring to the stage is
mad. Our chemistry is mad. It's straight energy. We both feed
off each other.

The way I work is a bit mad as well. Like, when we first
started working I remember writing down my set list like
fifteen minutes before a show. Or not even have a set list at
all. I'd play a tune, OK, calm. Then Stormzy would say a tune
and I'd have it there, ready. But back then I was also trying to
get equipment, trying to move professional in terms of being
on stage. We want to perfect it to the level where we know the
ins and outs, and we can never fail.

You're young, you want to link girls, go out partying and

all of that, but at the same time you've got to be grown. You've got to be on a bigger man ting. Because if you mess up, that's all on you.

The past three years have been a lot of work. I feel like I've been through the wave of #Merky and it's been mad. And now we're about to enter a new chapter. New things are happening. A new album is coming. Kaylum is directing. The shows are getting bigger. I've got my show on Capital now. I don't know where things are going, but I know I've got to work hard.

I don't want to be chilling. I don't take it for granted. I want to work as hard as I can. I can rest when I'm older.

Trevor

A few years ago the mainstream music industry probably just wanted to keep the grime scene in a little corner: 'Oh yeah, it's just them twenty or thirty guys on stage with a microphone and a DJ.' That was it.

The interesting thing is to see how well he's been received overseas, especially in Europe. To go to a show in Holland, say, and see the crowd rapping every word back to him is something special. There's a lot of love for him over there. They get it and they understand. They feel a part of it, and that's because he makes them feel a part of it.

You have a lot of people who make excuses for our success, rather than just see that we've grafted. Just do your graft, without trying to pull a man down. Think about the bigger picture. The scene could be so much bigger if everyone moved together.

Ayesha

He loves his fans, too. That's one of the main benefits of social media. He likes to engage with fans. He once received a tweet from a guy in a pub somewhere in London, who said, 'Stormzy! We're in Wetherspoons, come have a drink with us!' So Stormzy called up the pub and bought them a round, and said 'Sorry I can't make it, but have a drink on me.'

Flipz

Stormzy's been on it for a long time. His journey's been so mad. So much has happened. I'm just very grateful to have been a part of it.

The first couple of years completely opened my eyes. Different countries, different cultures, different food.

We never really had a south-side thing going on. That's why when I see youngers out there, I think: I know what you're going through.

Stormzy

Music is a crazy thing. The more I get into music, the more I understand. And the more surreal it gets. It's like Jay-Z rapping about the madness of fame, and I used to rap along, but it was only at a certain point that I really began to understand.

execution

Shoot my pain and slay my fear
Before I die I say my prayer
Don't worry about the mess, just leave me there.
This is all I got, so lay me bare.

'Lay Me Bare', *Gang Signs & Prayer*

introduction

Jude

By 2016 the team was established. Not only had they created a space for themselves within the industry, they were also starting to create something new. After the success of *Dreamer's Disease*, 'Know Me From' and 'Shut Up', Stormzy's abilities as an MC were undoubted. He was recognised as one of the most talented young grime stars of his generation. The problem was that he was trying to become something more than that.

For me, 'Shut Up' was a sign of Stormzy's artistry. Grime is a genre that is usually restricted in terms of its reach. There is a rawness and an abrasiveness to the music that is difficult to ignore. Grime lyrics can be violent, but they can also contain important messages. For an MC, it's how you choose to express your message that matters. Stormzy told me that he understands why people doubt or dislike his music. As long as the music is excellent, though, it will have something that's undeniable. And 'Shut Up', like so much of his music, was undeniable.

In 2016 it was time to take the next step. It was one the team had been working towards for a long time, and one that Stormzy had been planning for most of his life. It would be their biggest challenge yet. Having potential is one thing, but realising it is another.

After starting a number of tracks with various respected producers, Stormzy went into the studio to record his first album. Although he was still in regular contact with the team, it was a process that he would do alone, helped primarily by producer Fraser T. Smith, his sound engineer Manon Grandjean, and the musicians and artists who contributed to the album in one way or another. For ten months, Stormzy disappeared – sometimes entirely. There were periods when no one knew where he was, or what he was doing. But eventually, the album was finished.

Part 3 describes the creation of *Gang Signs & Prayer*, and the culmination of a lifetime of thinking about music. 'It's basically my story, from birth to twenty-three,' Stormzy says. 'I was thinking about the album for years and years. It's me personified.' The stakes were high: 'I wanted it to set the record straight . . . I wanted it to show the world that this is me.' An album to show what he was capable of as an artist, and to validate those who had faith in him. He also wanted to create a 'southside story', a true portrait of the ends, and of living in an area where opportunities were limited. An album to highlight the conflicts within the scene he had been embraced by, and within his life; the temptation to do wrong, and the struggle to do right. Growing up in south London was a wonderful yet troublesome experience.

Church seems to be the first piece of the puzzle. As Stormzy notes, the melodies that captivated him when he was young were found within hymns. Gospel music gave way to the nineties R&B his sisters played, and eventually to the first wave of grime – the music that was being championed by Alec and Austin, and was consumed by every member of the team, and by myself. But how do you reconcile those elements? How would it work?

And how would it be received? Considering how he was seen, as a talented young grime star more than anything else, Stormzy had more work to do than most. And being a young black man presents its own particular problems. Despite having a team that were fast becoming the envy of the industry, they also had to do it all themselves – the first time many of them had ever worked on a project of this scale. They had to find a way to get people to listen. They had the idea, and now they had to execute it.

In late January 2017, a series of posters appeared on billboards across London. They featured quotes, in white type on a black background, with the #Merky logo, an acronym and a date: '#GSAP 24:02'. I remember sitting in a friend's flat, around the corner from the Harris Academy where Stormzy went to school, and spotting one of the posters opposite. It said: 'All my young black kings rise up man, this is our year.' The message was captivating. I believed that it was our year.

7.

Stormzy

There are a lot of people who have helped me over the past few years. People I've learned from that have like-minded ambitions. People who want to do greater things. Ed Sheeran, for example. Ed has been a big help. We just clicked as soon as we met. He's my age, and he's just a normal guy who is achieving incredible things. I immediately saw someone who was doing what I wanted to do, in the way that he cares about his music, in what he's accomplishing as an artist, and in his work ethic. I see myself within this class of artist that also wants to achieve incredible things, so in everything I do I try to show excellence. I just want people to come away from my shows amazed, so I have to constantly up the levels. You need a lot of energy to pull that off. You need to work hard. I can't be tired. I can't even look tired. My body and my mind won't allow me to stay still.

Akua

I think the UK is an incredibly creative place. I think we do things that no other place does. We push boundaries.

It's ideas and it's execution. That's really all it is. I don't have a musical mind. But at the same time, what I do isn't that different to what everyone else does. It all boils down to ideas. We have ideas. That's how we operate. Not everything works, but everything is heard. And then when we find an idea that does work, our focus is on making it bigger or better or louder than what's come before. We have an idea and then we execute it.

Austin

I've always been a fan of new platforms, and new modes of music delivery, going all the way back to my mum having that computer in our house. VHS versus Betamax, CDs versus MiniDisc, MP3 versus WAV, and so on. I've also had a really good gauge of how the public's taste or mood is changing. So when streaming first came to the fore, I thought: Oh, this is really interesting, and kept an eye on what was happening. At a certain point in time, I could really smell a change in the air, both with the public and with the industry, and with the artist community as well, really. So when Spotify reached out to me, it felt like quite a natural transition. My day-to-day job wasn't going to be that different. I'd come in, listen to music, and the music I liked I would put on a playlist. What has changed is the process that you use. And the corporate environment. Bigger and older corporations tend to move slowly. Spotify was very forward-thinking, and very quick and nimble.

People tend to have a real misconception around data, as if Internet companies are the only people using data. If you're DJ TiiNY, and you're doing a set before Stormzy comes on, and you play a song and half the people in the audience stop dancing, that's you using data to see that there's a 50 per cent skip rate on that particular song. The difference is quality of data. It's a quality of data that's never been seen before. And what that means is that you make very informed decisions. But at the same time, there is other data. I remember being in Atlanta for work when 'Bodak Yellow' by Cardi B came out. And I was like, 'Yo! What the fuck is this tune, man?' So we found out what it was and put it on a few playlists in the UK. But when the data came back, it looked like no one was interested. I still thought that something might happen. The streaming data was weak, but the gut data was strong. So we kept the faith, and eventually we started to see the numbers improve, and it eventually became one of the Top 40 tunes in the UK. We use empirical data, and we use that feeling inside your belly, and that will never go away.

Alec (Twin)

Every relationship I've had with an artist is different. One of the most important parts of A&R is encouragement. Just being the person to say, 'Yes, what you're thinking is right,' and being a bit of a soundboard. It works both ways, as well. I'd play Stormzy music I was listening to, to get his take.

He respected my taste, and I think I had enough success on my own for him to respect what I was doing, and what I was about. I think he also respected the fact that I wasn't just chasing success in my work, but also quality, and things that had meaning and reason to exist. Finding the best thing, or helping to make something as good as it can possibly be.

He wanted to write great songs. Our relationship was very much about the music: how he sounds on a record, input on mixes, styles of producer, and the nuances of how to make a quality song. Real A&R nitty-gritty.

I knew from the beginning that we were always going to work together. And I knew that he was an intelligent person, and that he'd want to get a better understanding of how everything works and what's possible before making a decision. He was still making videos and freestyles, and so at that point he didn't really need a label.

I was just there to help, really. They were building momentum, and figuring out what they needed at each point, and they just thought, rightly: We can handle it. It's going to be stressful, it's going to be a lot of work, but we can handle it. My suggestion: Just make sure you get label services. Distribution and marketing and so on.

Stormzy

I'm just trying to make the greatest songs I can. I might be a bad-boy MC, and I'm a grime kid, and I know where I'm from, don't get me wrong. There was a time when I was just this south London grime kid. It was my area that was building me, and saying, 'Yo, world! Look at this guy!' I'll never forget it. I feel like my community is built on grime. My career is built on grime, but grime will do its own thing. My goal is to become an incredible artist, not just an incredible grime artist.

Saying that, the bottom line will still be the same. I'm still Stormzy. I'm still greazy. I'm still a bad boy.

Austin

I think our relationship has changed. Back when we met, what I could offer was the opportunity to have a song played. I'd say, 'Thank you for your song. I've now got to take it to my playlist meeting on Monday where I've got to try and convince ten other people that it's something that should be added to a playlist. If it gets through, it won't be played until the following Monday, as part of a playlist, for three minutes, to whoever is listening for those particular three minutes. And it won't be played again for another three hours, if you're lucky.'

Whereas now we can aim for a lot more. You can hold the record for the most amount of album streams in one week by a British artist. You can be the most streamed British artist on Spotify. You can have 250,000 people listening to your song right now. You can have tens of millions of streams all happening at the same time. The conversation goes from singular to plural. There are endless possibilities. Whereas I think with traditional media, there was only great potential. And don't forget, if enough people in that playlist meeting had said no, then Stormzy wouldn't have been played at all. Can you imagine? Or he wouldn't have been played until he'd really proven himself. But by then the picture might have looked very different.

It's the problem of gatekeepers. Now I'm out of it, the system looks very antiquated. Whereas with streaming, the audience decides. We have a team of editors who listen to music and pick out the diamonds, but we do it in the thousands, rather than the tens, and when we see something working, we're on it. And every single record is put on a playlist.

Gatekeepers in the traditional sense of the word control the absolute flow on their platform. So a gatekeeper in radio can stop an artist being played. They can stop their listeners from hearing that artist. At Spotify I'm more of a shepherd. The audience are already finding the music. My job is just to steer the music towards a particular audience in the shape of a playlist.

Our users are not one homogenous group. They're all different. Whereas gatekeepers hold the pipe, and release it, and hold it again, and the users have to take what's given to them, with us – it's a buffet. We're trying to bring some order to the chaos.

Stormzy

I'm trying to learn from the greats. Take Jay-Z, for example. He's taught me a lesson that I will never forget. Jay-Z is one of the last artists from his era still standing. He's not only standing up with the new kids, he's up with the new *new* kids. When 4:44 first came out, I was sceptical. I'm a Jigga fan, and I want to hear him spit all day, but I just thought: You've completed this shit! You are on the mountain top! It's done! You can't act like you're on the grind with us. And he didn't. All he did was speak his truth. It wasn't, 'Yeah, I'm in the club!' He was talking about his beef with the owner of Spotify, and his qualms with the CEO of Universal. He could talk about his relationship with Beyoncé. He could talk about his children. He could talk about what it's like to be a billionaire, and how he got there. That's why the album resonated. It's a classic album. It's his truth

Tobe

Having an ambition to make an album let me know that Stormzy had the ability to take his music to the next stage.

He's never started anything until he has a good idea about how to put it together.

After 'Know Me From', he thought: I'm ready to start thinking about my album. He knew which ingredients he needed to get started. He needed a way to sonically raise the bar for UK musicians. He wanted to work with live musicians, because he thought that was something UK artists weren't doing so much. He wanted to push the boundaries as much as possible.

Here's a secret: Stormzy was always playing around with the idea of a south-side story. Simply because he wanted to tell his story. He had twenty-three years of experience of a particular place, and that's what he wanted to get out.

For Stormzy it was never a case of whether or not he could show that side. He saw it as more of a duty. Not because he was popular or famous, but because he never found a source of that truth himself. Take *Gang Signs & Prayer*. A lot

of south London youth can relate to the title. They grew up
in very Christian households. But the push and pull of street-
level things, or money troubles at home, can lead you into
a different life. You live two lives, in fact. You do want that
relationship with God, and want God in your life, but you're in
an environment where most things are against you.

Fraser

I'm just a guy in a room, and I need to be sure that I can offer
something new each time I work with an artist. That's the only
way I can work. It's a different situation in the US – you hear
the same snares, and the same kick drums, again and again.
If you're hot over there, your beats can fly out of the door. But
you're hearing the same thing again and again. I've never
really worked like that.

I always want to feel like I've got something to bring to the
table. I'm not going to make 'P's & Q's' part 2. I've got to offer
something different. What I'm blessed with is a rich musical
background covering all genres. Kano was receptive to that.
We'd listen to lovers rock, Radiohead, reggae, all sorts. He
aspired to the highest heights, on his own terms.

Kano is a perfectionist, and a purist. He gets a beat to
the point where he loves it, however long it takes, and then
when it gets to the point where it's almost finished, he'll take
the beat away, and play it in his car on the very long journey
back home. Then he'll wake up in the morning and spit his
bars in the mirror. And keep doing it, again and again and
again. Eventually he'll come back to the studio, and walk into

the booth, and just perform it in one take. He'll perform for himself, but also for me. And it's one of the most exciting things you can witness.

Alec (Twin)

I always knew that making a great album was his number-one priority. I think he even mentioned it at our first meeting. He was definitely planning it a long time before that. We talked about it a lot – what he wanted to say, what I wanted to know, as a fan – but ultimately it's his album. That album was always in him. Certain concepts and ideas always existed. He mentioned the concept of 'Blinded by Your Grace' super early on. I just helped with some ingredients and was lucky enough to hear and feed back on some of the early brilliance that was happening.

Fraser, for instance. It took a while for them to connect, but when they did the timing was perfect. He had a lot of the pieces, but it was slightly fragmented, and it felt like a good way for it to happen was if he was working with someone who knew how to put albums together. How to make them work. Fraser is a genius and brings so much to the table for artists.

Fraser

Twin B was the link. And I'm eternally grateful to him for that. I'm a music fan, and I'm aware of all sorts of new music, just because I'm constantly listening to it. I think to be a good producer, you need to be a fan.

I'm a massive fan of UK hip hop and grime, and had

obviously spotted Stormzy, and could see him coming up. His star was rising but, if I'm honest, I wasn't sure what I could bring to the table. I'd just finished *Made in the Manor*, and I felt that I needed to do something different. We'd been in the studio on and off for eighteen months, and Kano had poured his heart into that record. I was so in that headspace. I needed to go away and try something else, so that I could offer something new. Maybe I needed to work with a band, or a solo artist. And I did say that, the very first time I met Stormzy. I said, 'I'm wary of repeating myself.' Unless you have time to reset, you fall victim to producing the same thing again.

I was quite upfront with Stormzy, but he said, 'Look, I'm going to attack this in a completely different way.' He was a fan of *Made in the Manor*, but he was equally attracted to the fact that I'd worked with Adele and Britney and various bands. The broadness, I guess.

There were a few things I noticed the first time I met Stormzy. His ambition, first and foremost. He had the same kind of ambition as Adele, and also the same kind of musicality. 'Know Me From' and 'Shut Up' were getting a lot of attention, but I knew him more as the person who'd made *Dreamer's Disease*. I knew the old Stormzy. I knew that he could sing. I knew his R&B roots. Stormzy has incredibly diverse tastes. One day he's drawing from a classical album, one day it's an old-school gospel track, or a saxophone refrain from *The Simpsons*.

I always looked to people like Rick Rubin in the US. He can say that he's worked with Johnny Cash and Jay-Z. He's worked with Black Sabbath and Eminem. He can look back and say that he's had a career in music. I want to be able to say the same. I'm strongest by bringing stuff in from Adele into Stormzy, and from Stormzy into Jon Bellion, and from Jon Bellion into Dave, and connecting those dots musically.

Stormzy

Before *Gang Signs & Prayer* I was an MC. I would just go to the studio and make something based on how I was feeling at that particular time. I couldn't describe it. I didn't really have the knowledge or the vocabulary to explain what I wanted to do. I would say I was a bit of a rough diamond. It got to the point where I thought my name was getting a bit bigger than my music. I was popping, but I didn't feel like I'd really done enough to deserve it. Twin told me to go and link Fraser, and to this day I think it's one of the most genius moves in my career. He could see my ambition, and my ideas, and my musicality, and he just thought: You need someone like Fraser.

Tobe

A few times we've seen artists not want to take certain steps because of the way things might be perceived. But I don't think you can ever make peace with your life if you can't be honest with yourself.

8.

Stormzy

The first time I met Fraser, we sat down and I said, 'OK, I want to make an album, and I want to call it *Gang Signs & Prayer*.' I started talking through some of my ideas, about the shape of the album, the sounds, the issues, the themes. He was just scribbling down notes, trying to keep up. The weird thing was, I didn't only have the album title, I also had titles for most of the songs. I knew that I wanted to make songs called 'Blinded by Your Grace' parts 1 and 2, to talk about my faith in God. At first we tried to make one song, and break it up. It was part 1, as it is now, plus some greazy rap verse. It just didn't work. 'Big for Your Boots' was always going to be in there, for years, so that was almost there.

I wanted to make a song called 'Mr Skeng' to show the world that when I pick up the mic to spit I'm not to be mistaken. I wanted 'Bad Boy' for anyone who thinks they're bad. I wanted 'Cigarettes & Cush' to talk about my relationship, and the joy and the love in my life; '100 Bags' about my mum. 'Velvet' was just me saying I love R&B and everything it embodies and how it makes you feel, and I wanted to emulate that. 'Lay Me Bare' and 'Don't Cry for Me', I just wanted to be honest, and vulnerable, and to bear it all with no fear or judgement.

With 'Return of the Rucksack', I wanted something that took me back. 'I was on my Saracen bike with the ridge back', or, 'I was on my BMX bike with the trick nuts' – that's exactly what I was doing. That's how I was getting around. And the chorus – 'I roll deep on these, / Put these MCs on deep freeze' – was exactly what I was listening to. I can't lie: musically, spiritually, I couldn't encapsulate that time any better than using Dizzee's 'Creeper' lyrics. That's exactly what I was listening to. That song was me personified, at a certain moment in time.

It's the same for GSAP. It's basically my story, from birth to twenty-three. I was thinking about the album for years and years. It's me personified.

I wanted to show all these sides of me. This is me. This is #Merky.

Fraser

The only way to get to know people properly is by spending time with them. My relationships with Stormzy, Kano and Dave are three of the dearest musical relationships I've ever had. I'm indebted to them for the music we've shared, but I'm also so close to them as people. Before Kano, I'd never spent ten months in a studio with anyone before. It makes such a difference, being with them every single day. You get to know them on their good days and bad days. You get to know their friends and family. You get to know them on a level that is beyond any other working relationship. And hopefully that comes through in the music. Stormzy took a chance on me, and I took a chance on him.

And with *Gang Signs & Prayer*, there was also the added pressure of producing something perfect.

Stormzy also has a grand vision. I realised quite quickly that the album was something that had to be perfect. He's a perfectionist. He had to get it right, however long it took. He would come up with lines in the studio, and perform to us as if it was a live show, to make sure that everyone in the control room was feeling it, and that it felt good to him too. He could record it in one take, but he preferred to go back again and again over every line to make sure it was perfect.

Manon

We worked together very closely in the studio, and so I quickly picked up how Fraser and Stormzy wanted things to sound. My role as the engineer was to understand their vision, and to try and capture everything that was happening in the studio, from Stormzy's vocals to the live instrumentation and all the programming. My job was also to marry everything together and find the balance between the real instruments and the programmed, so it sounds beautiful and raw at the same time. There were three key elements that we really focused on: the vocals, the live instruments and the drums.

In most grime tracks, the vocals are usually darker, sounding a bit more integrated within the track. Stormzy said he wanted his vocals to be clear and shine like a pop vocal. The vocal sound is a really important aspect of the whole album. Our task was to keep the toughness in some of the grimy songs, but also to have the vocals quite loud and proud and polished. Every time Stormzy went into the booth it was a bit of a mindblowing experience. He's got so much energy, and he's a perfectionist. Sometimes he would go into the booth and perform a song from the top until the end of the first take, but that would rarely be the final version. He'd listen back and redo sections again and again and again. He could tell immediately which parts weren't good enough, and would keep going over them until they were perfect. It was quite an intense process, because there is so much lyrical content and he is very fast and focused. He'd zero in on the smallest details, so I had to work hard to keep up.

Another interesting part of the process was to marry programmed grime beats with the live elements. It needed to sound different from other grime records, but it couldn't sound too live. The live instruments couldn't really wave around too much tempo-wise, it all had to be very tight with the drums to keep the toughness of the songs. Sometimes, after working on a song for a while, Stormzy would say, 'Shall we try a saxophone on this? Or a trumpet?' And Fraser would make it happen, and be able to work with the players so the parts fit the track. We even had a harp! The strings also became a bit of a secret weapon on some songs. We had live strings for 'Don't Cry for Me', 'Bad Boys', 'Mr Skeng' and

'Cold'. Even though they are not at the forefront , they bring so much to the tracks in my opinion.

As for the drums, Fraser spent a lot of time with Stormzy working on the beats, to make sure they were the right patterns, the right sounds, and that they also had the right swing, which was really important for Stormzy to flow over. Even the beats that came from different producers were tweaked so we could keep a coherent drums sound on the album.

Fraser

Stormzy's faith is important. He's driven by a higher source, and while our religious backgrounds may have been different, I think we connect on a spiritual level. A level of higher consciousness. 'Blinded by Your Grace, Pt. 2' was incredibly special. It was originally supposed to be a grime track. We were writing it late on a Sunday night, a very dark night, and the chords just came to me from nowhere. Or came to me from above. I'd never played those chords before. And Stormzy was in my live room writing the lyrics, and the bare bones of it were there. Then a day or two later MNEK came in and heard what we'd done, and started singing, and I just knew we had something very special.

Every track on the album is important to me. Every track was a journey. I remember when Kehlani's vocals arrived for 'Cigarettes & Cush', and they were absolutely perfect. Or when Ghetts came in and did his thing. Or Hus, working through the night. Or when Stormzy shared the voicemail from his mum. All very special memories.

Before we started the album process, Stormzy had been making a lot of tracks with some incredible producers. It wouldn't have been that record without them – Sir Spyro, Sunny Kale, Mura Masa, Wizzy Wow, Swifta Beater, EY, Sons of Sonix. I've been talked about as the guy who made that record with Stormzy, which is true, but as well as starting tracks from scratch, we also started with some great beats from these guys, and then worked with amazing musicians, singers and arrangers such as Rosie Danvers, Ben Epstein and Dion 'Chord Lord' Wardle to perfect it.

Manon

His work ethic is incredible. He'd be in the studio for as long as it would take. And sometimes he'd just stop by to spend an hour recording vocals with me. He's very strong-minded as well, and knows what he wants, and what he doesn't want. He also knows when a song is not quite good enough, so him and Fraser would brainstorm and work on it to bring it up to the level of the others, or scrap it if it didn't work and start again. I think it takes a lot of courage to do that, to be so certain in your ideas. It's quite scary throwing songs away, but he knew what he was doing. It was one of his strengths, for sure.

'Blinded by Your Grace, Pt. 2' was a totally different song, originally. It was a grime track. But Stormzy didn't think it was working. He said, 'I'm not feeling this.' So he started from scratch again, jamming with Fraser, and they came up with something else, which is the track how we know it now. And then MNEK came in and produced all these beautiful vocals. He went into the booth after listening to the track a couple of times, and started singing all these ad-libs, and would layer harmonies one after the other without even listening to what he'd recorded on the previous takes. It was incredible.

Another highlight was when J Hus came in to do his bit on 'Bad Boys'. He came in at ten or eleven at night, with five or six guys. We just looped his section, and he sat down and started writing his bars silently. Then after a while he stood up and said, 'All right, I'm ready,' went into the booth, and just blew everyone away. So did Ghetts!

Stormzy

I was in the studio for ten months, and there were times I wasn't really talking to anyone. I was mad depressed for a while, and going through a lot of shit. But I just disappeared for ten months. People were asking all sorts. What's going on in there? Has he gone pop? Is he keeping it super grimey and greazy? No one knew.

I was a bit of a nightmare, I won't lie. We'd have some great days in the studio, making 'Cold' or 'Cigarettes & Cush', and then I'd ghost. I'd just be sitting in my house. No one would see me for days, or weeks. Recording an album is a soul-baring process. It's not easy. I might come back to the studio for a little while, and have a long conversation with Fraser, and work on a few tracks, but then I'd disappear again.

I was going through so much while I was making the album, and I was overwhelmed. My career has had so many turning

points. Back then I was just getting used to fame. Struggling
to become Stormzy. Trying to adjust to living in a new area.
Having money. Family issues. Making an album. Even before
the album I wasn't really coping, so add the album to it all, and
the pressure I put on myself, and you can perhaps understand
why it wasn't easy. I was so broken-spirited. When I was in the
zone, I was flying, but I'd have some serious lows.

Alec (Twin)

Making a debut album is a really, really daunting process. You
could tell from the times when he just disappeared that it was
understandably overwhelming at moments.

Fraser

I could see at times when he came in that he wasn't feeling
it. I never tried to pressure him. There were dips, like when
his friend committed suicide. There were periods over the
summer of 2016 when he wouldn't come out of his house or
answer his phone.

The most important question for me was 'Is he OK?' As a
friend, that was my priority. All I could do was to text him and
check he's OK, and say that I was there for him.

There was also the practical side of things. I had a studio
to run and an engineer to pay, and I wasn't going to work with
anyone else during this period. I was in the GSAP headspace.

There was also a bit of paranoia. I was worried that he wasn't
happy with the tracks. We'd spent six or seven months on the

album by this point, and we hadn't really discussed it. I didn't know what was going on. It's testament to my relationship with him that I was never going to walk away. I knew that what we had created was great, and that the project was incredibly important. It might sound like bullshit – it's very easy to say it after the fact – but I knew I had to do it, and that I had to stand by him. I remember my wife, Sarah, asking if we could go away on holiday, but I just knew Stormzy was coming back. And he did.

While he was in this dark space, he'd obviously been working out some personal issues, but he'd also been listening to the album. We looked at the whiteboard, and rubbed a lot of tracks off. I write something like two hundred songs a year, but only forty make it. People will judge me on the stuff that's released, but I wish they could see the hard drive! But that's why the stuff that does come out is of a certain level. Sometimes you're only as good as the stuff you don't release.

When Stormzy returned for the final push, there was a feeling of clarity that we both suddenly had, and we were able to take it over the line. It took us another three months, but we did it.

Flipz

There were times during the making of the album when I wouldn't hear from him for a while. He would bounce back and get back in the studio, but he was really going through some stuff.

He knew what he wanted the album to sound like. First and foremost, a guy from the ends who's gone through bare fuckeries. How we live in south London, and him being depressed, and also his faith.

He worked hard. He spent two or three days on 'Cold', just making sure it was perfect. The same with 'Velvet'. Or flying to New York to get the choir for 'Blinded by Your Grace'. He's constantly observing what other artists are doing. So he'd go to an Adele show, or an Ed Sheeran show, and come back with new ideas. Or Kendrick at Coachella. That was eye-opening. It's looking at what works, and what doesn't.

Tobe

It's like, we've worked with some artists who have agreed not to take an advance. Most artists would fight for an advance. It's the sensible thing to do. There's no way of knowing if the track will sell, if you'll see any money down the line. But another view was: Well, if there is no money from it, that's fine. I believe in the music. What it means to be on the album is more important. So if Stormzy wants me on the album, let's not talk about an advance.

Stormzy

God made it very clear to me what I had to do. I knew what it should be, and I knew how I should be to get that result: very meticulous, very selective, very exacting. And that's down to God.

With *Gang Signs & Prayer*, I wanted people to feel it. 'First Things First' is a statement of intent. I want you to know

I mean business. The second track, 'Cold', was a message
of skill, flow, confidence, and an opportunity for me to get
things off my chest. I just wanted to say,

All my young black kings rise up man, this is our year
   And my young black queens right there
It's been a long time coming, I swear

I wanted to say that. And I wanted to say 'a young black boy
made a milli off grime'. Like, a *young black boy* made a million
pounds from grime. That's got to mean something.

And then 'Blinded by Your Grace'. That was going to be one
track. It was going to move from the chorus into me spitting,
but we tried it and it was dead. We split it into two and it started
to work. I knew I had to sing it, but I tried it in the studio and
my voice wasn't quite there. It's such a beautiful song, and so
polished, and my voice wasn't doing it justice. I was feeling
it, the emotion was there, but it wasn't polished. I'm not the
greatest singer. I then got a young up-and-coming singer named
Deno who I had seen on Instagram to cut the vocal, for it to
maybe work as a sort of interlude or a stand-alone track, but I
scrapped that idea down the line as well. Eventually I realised
that the only way to protect the purity of the song, and to
execute a song of this purity with my somewhat sub-par vocal,
was to do it live. So we did. Got Yasmin Green to come along
and keep me in check. We just recorded it. Got it done.

Then 'Velvet'. I wanted to make a straight-up R&B tune, that's
so fly, and so melodic, and so sweet and just touches your soul.
Then I heard NAO's song 'Intro (Like Velvet)', and I just thought:

Wait, this shit's too short! I DMed her and said, 'That song's too short! How dare you make this song so short!' She's one of my favourite artists ever, and her voice is so beautiful, but it was just too short. I wanted to make something that made girls feel sweet and something that made the mandem feel smooth.

How would you feel if a brother stayed around?
Taking care of you and not the other way around?

I wanted it to be euphoric, I wanted people to feel something. After I heard NAO's 'Intro' I just thought that we could also make an ode to an incredible black British singer at the same time. And get Jenny Francis to come and bring the mood, because Jenny Francis is a legend. She used to have a show on Choice FM that was legendary for my older sister's generation, and I always used to listen when my sister was tuned in. So I knew what it'd mean to not only my sister, but to a whole generation of people to have her bless the album, and to also school the younger lot!

I tried to sing it myself first. I heard it back, and I was like: No, Stormzy, that's never going to work, bro. You're never going to be able to carry that emotion as well as her, so let her do it. Focus on your own part. I was learning to make music.

Then it goes into 'Mr Skeng', and I'm shelling down on a Spyro riddim. With 'Mr Skeng' I just wanted to take it old school. 'Dickhead yout and a dickhead crew getting gassed up by your dickhead friends' – that was just how I felt at the time. I just thought: Bro, I've got to be Mr Skeng for one moment. Talking to all your MCs. This is all your smoke. Just getting things off my chest. Saying something back to the naysayers. Oh, I can't be the king of grime because I can't do radio sets?

> I do rap then I do grime then I do rap then
>   I sing then I go right back
> They said 'You ain't gonna blow like that?!'
> Who gives a fuck you know like that.

I'm a hungry young don in the studio. For years I've been listening to Frank Ocean, James Blake, Adele, Kanye West. I've got so many ideas. There's a version of 'Cigarettes & Cush', for example, that has an extra refrain after the chorus – 'you don't ever let me down', and then strings, before I'd come back in and rap. I just wanted to be a smooth motherfucker. When I was recording it, I thought: Yeah, this is hard. But then I played it back and I thought: Um, no, not really. I realised I need someone like Kehlani, who's got the smoothest voice in the world. We ended up with thirty-one different versions of that song.

It was a bit mad. In the studio, I'd hear the riddim and I'd just say to Fraser, 'Play it again. Play it again. Play it again.' Everyone would look at me like I was crazy, but I could hear something. There was a clash in the cymbals, or something. I learned to pick up on the tiniest things.

Fraser

The track listing was a major part of the process, and took us a lot of time to perfect. We didn't want to front-load it with

3. execution

Studio life, part 1.

Studio life, part 2.
With live players,
and Ed Sheeran and
Fraser T. Smith.

The countdown begins.

Team #Merky on the campaign trail.

Number one.

he first shows.

GSAP, Dublin and London, 2017.
Yeah I'm Abigail's yout but I'm God's
son.' 'Blinded by Your Grace, Pt. 2'.

Glastonbury, 2017.

'I stay prayed up
then I get the job
done.' 'Blinded by
Your Grace, Pt. 2'.

bangers. The only tune that people had heard up to this point
was 'Shut Up', which we'd thought should go towards the end.
I remember listening back to the album one day, and Stormzy
said, 'You know what? I want to put "Blinded by Your Grace,
Pt. 1" as track four.' I thought: OK. So we're starting off with
'First Things First', which is a hard opener, and then into
'Cold', which is a straight-up grime track, and then into 'Bad
Boys' with J Hus and Ghetts, then we drop 'Blinded by Your
Grace, Pt. 1', which is an interlude, and very stripped back.
I wasn't sure. It didn't feel like the right moment to put in a
track like that – something very different, something acoustic,
and something that's extremely personal. You'd normally opt
for something safe. But he did it. And he sang it! He not only
sang it, but he sang it live, in a room full of extraordinary
singers. He bared his soul. That's how you achieve greatness.
It goes beyond a beat, or strings. If it's real, it touches
people's souls.

Tobe

I couldn't be in the studio. I have too many opinions,
and I'm too much of a music fan to keep quiet. It wouldn't
have been productive. I always said to Stormzy, 'Don't
play me anything unless you're absolutely sure about it.
Because if you're not, and I give you my honest opinion,
then it could send you in the wrong direction. If you
really like it, then it becomes more of a constructive
conversation.'

Kaylum

I documented the whole process. The recording of songs: 'Bad Boys', 'Mr Skeng'. One day with a whole orchestra there. J Hus coming by. Filming the posters going up. All of it.

His main thing with videos is the fans. He loves his fans. He'd always try to give something back somewhere. Back in the day, he'd always arrange things for his fans – come down to his videos, spit on his cypher.

Take the 'Blinded by Your Grace' video, for example. He wasn't just asking fans to be involved, he was checking on them all, making sure they were all right, that they were happy.

Stormzy

I remember when I first mentioned to people that I was working with Fraser, there were a few questions. Like I was about to turn pop. But I had a clear idea of what I wanted to achieve, and I knew he had things to teach me. I'm so grateful to him for his wisdom, and his patience. He knew when to give me space, and when to push me, and I'll be forever grateful.

Those ten months were the craziest times of my life. At the time it was gruelling, it was fun, it was mad. I was this twenty-two-year-old kid with some mad ideas, and he made it happen.

I had to make a body of work to show the world 'This is me.' And I'm going to do it again and again. Man's going to produce another body of work that, God willing, the world is waiting for. People say, 'Was it a fluke?' and I'm like, 'Bro, I haven't even started yet.'

Tobe

Stormzy is the narrator, but it's not just his story. He never wanted it to be the life of Stormzy. Everyone's experienced it, but no one's talking about it. So, for example, a West African background, Christian parents, the struggles of growing up in south London knowing that there are so many things against you, and so on. He had the opportunity to speak for so many people, so always knew that the album would never just be for him. He's very aligned with people like himself. As much as I get to experience this, there is a reality that I faced that so many people like me still face, and it can't be ignored. We have to show that we can do this. People are seeing themselves in him. So he has to fight to show people what can be done. What can be done when you focus and work hard and don't let the doors close.

9.

Fraser

For those ten months, it was just me, Stormzy, Flipz, Rimes and my engineer Manon who had heard the album. At the end of the process, it was like we were arm in arm, on the edge of a cliff. If we'd got it wrong, then we'd made a huge mistake. But if we'd got it right . . .

Manon

It was quite a scary moment when the album was finished. Fraser and I had spent so much time on every single detail of every single song that it was really hard for me to step back and just listen to it all without worrying about the work I'd done. The process got quite intense towards the end. We were up against a tight deadline and we were mixing the record while still recording quite a lot of it.

The first time I could enjoy it properly was at the listening party we had at the studio. Fraser and Stormzy invited a group of friends in, and we just listened to the mastered album the whole way through. Nobody would ever know that a particular bridge had taken a hundred takes to get right, or that we'd spent hours making edits to one of the songs. It was just good to listen to it, and to see everyone loving it. It was a very emotional moment for me for sure.

I think we knew – or hoped – that the album was going to do well, but we had no idea it would be so successful.

Stormzy

In this British musical landscape, being a black artist making black music is hard. I think that's partly due to the fact that there aren't many black people in positions of power within the music industry. It's a bit better now, but when I started out, it wasn't so good. Austin and Twin were there. It's difficult to describe their roles, back then. They were more like family. They were in positions of power, but they cared about me. They cared enough about the culture, and cared enough about me as a young black man to be there whenever I needed, in whatever capacity.

Austin has always been there, even going back to the 1Xtra days. And Twin's like a mentor. Twin's a teacher, but he talks to you as a peer, or colleague, or music man to music man. I've had the best music conversations with Twin. He helped me to develop my musical vocabulary. We might be discussing a track, and I'd be describing particular elements, and Twin would say something like, 'The truth in that song . . . ,' and we'd have a conversation about truth in music, and it would open my eyes to truth as a quality in music, and something to strive for.

The funny thing about Twin is that the A&R relationship has only just begun. It's only in the last couple of months that we've been working on music together. He was the first person to hear *Gang Signs & Prayer* in full, apart from Fraser and Manon. But he didn't hear it until it was finished. For a long time there were rumours flying around that I'd secretly signed to Atlantic, but the truth was I was just close to Twin. Atlantic might have wanted to sign me, and Twin might have been a part of that, but we just discussed music. And then he was the first person I wanted to hear it. I remember him saying, 'You've done it.' That was it.

Alec (Twin)

I heard *Gang Signs & Prayer* and ÷ on the same day. It was weird. We went to a bar nearby to listen to ÷ with Ed, and then I drove over to Fraser's place to listen to *Gang Signs & Prayer*. Two game-changing albums on the same day. It was mad.

I never asked Stormzy anything about it before I heard it, and there were so many rumours floating around about certain superstars being in the studio, different MCs, guest producers, etc. I just thought: When he's ready, we'll talk. A part of me wanted to slip back into fan mode. So I could be pure about my opinion. But it was now past that because the album had potentially become so important to the musical landscape of our era. Past some of the excellent demos and ideas . . . What does this now super-important album sound like?

I remember arriving at Fraser's and meeting Stormzy, and as we walked in he let out another heavy sigh. I could tell he was really nervous. They had spent so long making it, putting love, care and passion into it.

Fraser

I'll never forget the moment we played the record to Twin B. Don't forget, he was the person that connected us. Just playing it to him, and seeing his reaction. And playing it to Austin Daboh, who's been such an influential figure, and such a torch-bearer of black culture. I think it's fair to say that he was speechless, when we got to the end of the record. He was saying he hadn't heard anything as strong since Dizzee's *Boy in da Corner*. I felt a mixture of awe, at his comments, but also huge relief.

Akua

I knew he was recording, I knew it was coming together, but I didn't know it was finished until he called up and said, 'The album's ready! Come round and hear it.'

There's ten years between me and Stormzy, so when I went into the studio, I thought that maybe the music he's making for him and for his generation might not be for me. It doesn't mean I can't enjoy it, it doesn't mean I don't like it. It's just not targeted at me. But when I heard it I was so surprised. I wasn't expecting it. It was a bit of a revelation. When I heard 'Cigarettes & Cush', and 'Velvet', and 'Blinded by Your Grace',

I thought: The job we have to do isn't the one I was expecting to do. Actually, a lot of it will be getting people to listen to it so that they can understand how different it is. And how different it is to what they thought it was going to be.

DJ TiiNY

It was 2017, and I was thinking: Cool, man's going to bring out an album soon. I was at home, in the ends. Just chilling with the mandem. Then it dropped.

It was a like a movie. 'First Things First' was explosive. It was like he was saying, 'Bro, this is who I am. Respect what I'm doing. Follow me.' I was smiling when I heard it. He took it his own way.

I could immediately see how it could be performed. He likes to adopt a persona on stage, and you can see how he'd perform every track. 'Velvet', 'Cigarettes & Cush', 'Big for Your Boots' – it was all there. And these aren't hard grime tracks, but they've got that hood sound. And they're smooth. He's expressing his feelings. He wasn't sticking to one genre. It was a tribute to his influences. It's not a grime album, it's a Stormzy album. He sprays facts. He tells stories. Wiley, Kano, Skepta are all the same. It's like 'Blinded by Your Grace' – he's taking us to church. Certain man can play it in their car on a Sunday and that's their service.

Trevor

I had no idea what the album was going to sound like. The first time I heard anything about it was when Stormzy messaged me to see if I could find some gospel singers. I had no idea what he was up to.

The first time I heard the album I just thought: Damn. It had everything! Grime, singalongs, R&B and gospel. I can't lie, I was absolutely taken aback by what Stormzy had created, and couldn't wait to put it together live. It already sounded like a live show itself.

When it came out I was just playing it constantly. I was working on the tour at the time but I'd still have it on all the time in the car, at home, wherever I happened to be.

Tobe

He writes a lot of his music on his own, just thinking about what he wanted to say, and how he wanted to say it. He wasn't watching anyone else. He didn't add a feature because someone was popular. The influences were his own. He was speaking about what mattered to him, not what was on the news at the time. He had to put it together himself.

But at the same time, it's so universal. The first time I heard it, I said, 'Did you make this for me?' Because I was sure he was responding to things we had talked about, and things I was praying for. Like with '100 Bags': it connects so closely with my experience growing up, and how I feel about my mum, but in actual fact I'd never really spoken to him about that. He just wrote it.

Flipz

I really didn't want to listen to it for a while. I wanted to listen to it when everyone else got to listen to it, but because I was with him constantly, I picked it up. And I think it's an album that's going to go down in history. I genuinely do. It's going to be remembered. And as he drops more music, he's only going to get better, and better, and better.

Rachel

The first song I heard was 'Big for your Boots', and I remember thinking, this is sick. 'This has got to be a single,' I said to him. He then played me 'Cold' and I know at one point there was a brief conversation between Tobe and him on whether to go out with 'Cold' or with 'Boots' first. It was in a state of flux for a while.

Stormz later told me that were a lot of songs that were on the record at one point, and then taken off of it, and there were also others that came in late. 'Lay Me Bare' was laid down last – that track really had me – it was an extraordinarily brave song and he gave it everything. It was a 'Before I finish, I need everyone to know this' type song. Then the album was done.

I listened to it on repeat. One night I was on the Tube, thinking of how many poignant and important lyrics were on the record: 'Crikey! Oh my god it's Big Mikey', 'All my young black kings, rise up man, this is our year'. I said to him and Tobe at the #Merky Christmas dinner, 'What are your thoughts on placing some billboards – with these lyrics on – around London to tease the debut album?' Stormzy had been away for some time and we needed to launch in a fairly non-traditional way. And that was the beginning of the GSAP promo timeline – the campaign had begun. The months ahead were challenging but when you look back on it, what a flippin' year it was.

During the early stages of me joining the team, I soon learnt that the ethos is, and will always be, that anything could be possible. That impacted my way of thinking when I came to planning the PR around the album.

We all knew the primary objective was to reach number one on the chart, thus becoming the first ever grime album to do so, but in essence, GSAP pushed boundaries before it had even been released. Yes, Stormzy can do grime. But he can also do gospel, he can sing, he can harmonise and in turn we needed to showcase his versatility across all aspects of the promo campaign, too.

Stormzy ripping up the industry rule book became the central element of my pitches. I wanted him to grace magazine covers that he deserved to grace and to me it was crucial that we broke him out of specialist media and into the mainstream. And Stormzy's aspirations were – and will always be – very much the same. Not even close to what many a journalist or broadcaster thought they may be. I felt that one of the main problems from outside of the scene looking in was pigeon-holing, and it was important we helped overcome the stereotypes.

Style press for example, was sadly a fairly untouched area when it came to grime musicians in 2015 and 2016, and so I made it my mission to have them on board and for them to understand the importance of this man. Soon enough, he was gracing the pages of GQ, Esquire and the cover of i-D. And also FADER, which was one of the magazines Stormz highlighted to me as one he wanted to be on the cover of from day one. Within the music world, gracing that cover is a big deal – and so it had to happen. He also wanted to be on the cover of British GQ and after the success of #GSAP, they conceded. He was the first British MC to be on their cover in over 5 years.

The PR strategy was to build on his fan base – but never to ostracise his current fans – and to broaden it. Another was to have him attend a lot of key events. My thing was, not only could this young king star on the cover of these fashion magazines, but he could affiliate himself within the mainstream and was present at some of the most prestigious events. Soon enough, 'Brand Stormzy' was expanding.

He's aided me to grow into the person I am today. Working with him changed the way I work completely. It's encouraged me to learn, to push myself and explore other ways of creating conversations. Traditional PR will never be a thing with him.

Tobe

The album proved that you can't call Stormzy a one-category artist. He's very aware of his influences, and the fact that there are lots of different things he would like to represent in his music. In the end, I think he found the best thing to do was to be truthful. If he wasn't honest, it would be very easy to pull the album apart. If you saw him in a video flashing money and jewellery and talking about Thornton Heath, you wouldn't believe him.

He made a track with Little Mix, for example. In our minds, the song was a good song, first and foremost. There was a lot that Stormzy wanted to talk about, too. He's probably not the first person you think of when you hear the word feminist. But you have to remember that he was raised by his mother. He was educated by his two older sisters. He has always believed in equality, and he believed in the song's message. So it felt like an opportunity to speak to something that really mattered to him, that celebrates and elevates women and the women in his life, in some way. But also, we were thinking: Why can't we do it? Why can't we record a song with the top girl band in the country, if not the world? Why is it something to be ashamed of? Why would I worry about looking moist? The way you think people perceive you can stop you from taking certain steps that might actually be progress.

He also called me up when he'd finished making 'Cigarettes & Cush', and he said, 'I think I've made a banger, but I'm also shook, because I just don't know how people are going to take it.' I said, 'Your real fans will know you've got range. It's going to be a harsh transition for some people.' And it was. You saw it when we released the album. People said, 'What the fuck is this? He's sold out!'

Ayesha

Stormzy doesn't like to be boxed in. Because he's so creative, he's constantly changing. Ultimately it's about the music, but with GSAP he said, 'It's not a grime album, it's not a gospel album, it's not a rap album. We'll just make it, put it out, and it's up to the individual to find their own perspective on it.'

He does a lot that goes under the radar. He doesn't like to announce things. He just wants to do it and be authentic and from the heart. It's his faith in God that inspires him.

Akua

My focus was how we could use the relationships we'd built to support the album launch. So, one of the first conversations I had was with Red Bull, who sponsored the pop-up show on the first album launch day. It was a lot of hard work but we had a great first day, and ended up in Box Park in Croydon. It was huge.

And we were also speaking to Adidas, and did an event in store with signings, and we were speaking to Manchester United as well, who were so down to try anything. I just sent them a big wishlist and thought they'd say no to everything, but they didn't. Basically we just had to get Mourinho to sign off on it! So we went to the training ground and met the players in the morning. That was a bit tight. Mourinho had only said yes at 11 p.m. the night before. And then we went to the megastore and 700 people turned up. Stormzy is still the only non-footballer to have held an event at the Old Trafford megastore. And then we gatecrashed a Sky interview with

Michael Carrick, as he'd just announced his testimonial. That went down quite well.

I was checking the sales figures while all of this was going on, and seeing that we were behind where we wanted to be. And when the conference ended Luke Shaw and Ashley Young walked out and said hello, and asked how we were doing. I told them, and I remember Luke saying, 'Don't worry, you'll be fine.' But I wasn't sure.

There was also a sense that people didn't want this to happen. People didn't want this for us. While we were at the training ground, Tobe had been getting all these emails from the chart people saying that they were pulling our numbers. It was so disheartening but, if anything, it just made us more determined to do it. We're independent, we're doing everything ourselves, and we're paying for everything ourselves. We're trying to pave a new way. And there were people who were so invested in bringing us down. It was a really weird one for me. Everyone will always tell you it's not personal. You've just got to keep doing your own thing.

Austin

We gave the album a lot of support. We really wanted to make a statement that Spotify is here and we can support urban artists as well as other platforms. We had a TV campaign around the Brit Awards, we had a billboard campaign, and he benefited from a vast amount of support globally from the editorial teams. By the time it came out, we could really do no more. If the album had come out and hadn't done what we were hoping it would, we would have pulled back our support. We don't just throw the kitchen sink at someone and leave it, because we like them. We have to follow the users.

So the album came out on Friday. And we were starting to get the numbers through the next day, Saturday afternoon. A good number for a first day is 500,000 streams. For an unsigned British artist, 500,000 would be very good indeed. A million would be fantastic.

Akua

The release week was intense. I'd never done anything like it before. I was broken. The whole campaign had been so rapid. We'd been making decisions to do things and turning everything around in hours. My body was not moving. There was so much running around. After the trip to Manchester some of the boys took a car home and I was on the train, and I just felt like there was really nothing more we could have done. I thought: Regardless of what happens, we have to be proud of it.

Everyone was rooting for us, too. I had so many people in the industry texting me, asking where we were. What did we need to do? What else was there? We had so much goodwill behind us it felt like we had to win.

Tobe

Week one of the album launch, we were posting tweets asking people to stream, because we were so close to doing it. And apparently there's a grey area in the rules for the Official

Edgware Library
Tel: 020 8359 2626
Email: edgware.library
@barnet.gov.uk

Borrowed Items 11/02/2020 11:25
XXXXXXXXXX4165

em Title	Due Date
A marvelous life : the mazing story of Stan Lee	03/03/2020
Bitcoin billionaires : a true tory of genius, betrayal and edemption	03/03/2020
Unicorn : the memoir of a luslim drag queen	03/03/2020
uro noir : the pocket ssential guide to European rime fiction, film TV	12/02/2020
ecrets of the Lost symbol : e unauthorised guide to e mysteries behind	12/02/2020
ollected stories	12/02/2020
ohn le Carre : the ography	12/02/2020
orn to run	12/02/2020
on	12/02/2020
he crime writer's casebook a reference guide to police vestigation past	12/02/2020
merican girls : social edia and the secret lives of enagers	12/02/2020
ama's boy : a memoir	12/02/2020
Vhite	12/02/2020

Amount Outstanding: £0.25

ndicates items borrowed today
hank you for using this unit

Charts around pushing people to buy music directly, so the Official Charts deducted a number of our sales.

We were in number-one position, and then we lost it. We were in the car on the way home from Manchester, listening to the album again, resigned to the fact that we weren't going to make it. Stormzy's lyric came on, 'I stay prayed up and then I get the job done,' and he said, 'Look, we've done everything we can. It's Thursday night, we can't tweet any more, we can't tell our people to stream, or buy the album. The next part is really up to God.'

Flipz

The day we got the sales figures was a bit mad. We were up in Liverpool to sign CDs, then over to Old Trafford to meet the Man United players, then back to London. It was in the car on the way back that we discovered that Rag'n'Bone Man had overtaken us. He'd sold, like, 5,000 more CDs. The mood in the car changed instantly. I just went to sleep. I couldn't take it. We all wanted it as much as Stormzy.

A bit later we were listening to GSAP in the car, 'Blinded by Your Grace, Pt. 2', and he said, 'I think we've got it, you know.' I was like, 'Bruv, do you know something I don't? We've just been overtaken!' We got back home, and were sitting outside his house talking, and he was still saying, 'Don't worry, bruv, we've got it.' I wasn't sure. I still had fear in me.

Akua

So eventually I got home and just went straight to bed.
I woke up at six in the morning and remember thinking
immediately: Have we done it? So I texted Stormzy, and for a
while there was no response. Then a text appeared: 'AK we've
fucking done it! But don't tell anyone.' I was like: What? Don't
tell anyone! I was jumping around my flat screaming. Then
I called Tobe and I swear he might have been crying. 'AK,
we've done it!'

Flipz

The next day, I got a FaceTime from Stormzy. If he ever
FaceTimes me, I know it's either very good news, or very
bad news. We've broken a record, or someone's died. That's
it. I was just lying in bed awake, thinking about the day
ahead. So I waited for a moment, and answered it. He was
like, 'Bro, we got it! We fucking got it!' It was such a good
feeling. Because I don't think he could have heard number
two. I don't think I could have heard it. It wasn't acceptable.
God has a plan for us, of course, but it would have knocked
his confidence. So I hopped out of bed and took a train to
his house. We were drinking champagne, just chilling.
Listened to it on the *Official Chart* show, went to see everyone
at ADA, came back home and Ed Sheeran popped round.
It was mad.

Rachel

The day Stormzy got the number one chart position I lost my mind. That week had been so intense, all of us – Stormzy especially – were completely drained. If he wasn't flipping pancakes with Raymond Blanc for a GQ live stream he was signing CDs at Man U's training ground. If he wasn't there, he was sitting on BBC Breakfast sofa, or performing a few album tracks at a surprise show in Westfield. We did everything we possibly could to promote this record.

We'd been number one in the midweeks all week and then the Thursday morning, the charts came in and we'd been overtaken by Rag'n'Bone Man and we were heartbroken . . . I remember my mate Jackie stayed at my house the night before the final chart position because I hadn't been sleeping that week – none of us had! I called Stormz late that night and he was with Flipz and he just said to me, 'We've got it, I just have a feeling we have got it.' In the morning Jackie and I got an Uber to work with my housemate Max in case I got a call relating to the charts. I remember being in the Uber when the GM from ADA – the distributor of GSAP – called me with Tobe already on the line. He said, 'We've done it.' I said, 'What? We've done it?' I punched the roof, screamed my lungs out and cried all in the same breath. Coincidentally, the Uber was pretty close to Stormzy's house so I got out and just ran to his place. That feeling was euphoric, I was so happy and so unbelievably proud of him. I just knew how much this meant to him, to us, to the scene.

Within British culture, so many artists paved the way and

built the foundations, but it was Stormzy who opened the floodgates. I don't believe there could or would have been a number one grime album before Stormzy.

Tobe

I'd seen people's calculations online, but I didn't find out the numbers until someone from the Official Charts Company called me to tell me. I was so happy. It seemed like everyone was happy, too. It just felt like there was a real force behind it. It felt like people wanted it, and people were a part of it. Whenever I saw someone that week they didn't say congratulations, they were saying, 'We did it. It was us.' And that was the goal.

Kaylum

It's an album for everyone. An album is your soul. When I first heard it, I thought: This guy is just going to be the best thing in the world. He's going to be a legend. He already is a legend.

After it came out, we were checking the sales every day. When I heard we were number one it was mad. He was doing everything he could do. His head was on fire.

Austin

I remember I was at home, and a colleague called me and said, 'Have you seen the Stormzy numbers yet?' On its first day, *Gang Signs & Prayer* did 4.7 million streams. 4.7 million.

At that moment we knew it was going to be something special. We're about to break some records here. And by the time we got to Wednesday, it had clocked 19 million streams in the UK. Stormzy's first-week numbers were rivalling and in some cases breaking those of Adele, Ed Sheeran, Taylor Swift, Drake, The Weeknd, Bruno Mars. And that in itself is incredible. He was the biggest-ever solo artist and most-listened-to British artist. Every single from *Gang Signs & Prayer* was in the Top 40.

Alec (Twin)

When I heard it was number one I must have screamed for about an hour. I remember Austin called me, and I just screamed.

Ayesha

I remember the night GSAP got to number one. I was away on holiday, but I was glued to my phone. Everyone wanted them to win.

The whole team's vibe was, give it all up to God. Whatever way it goes, God's got us. If we're meant to be number two, then we will just go harder next time – but it didn't happen that way.

DJ TiiNY

The album came out and it went gold in two weeks. I just remember thinking: This is actually happening to us. This is us. If man put in work like this and has achieved this level of success, then what comes next?

It was perfect. And I think it changed a lot of people's perspective on what's possible in music. Hopefully it goes beyond music. It's the same with the team. Hopefully what we're doing will help a new generation of managers coming up, a new generation of DJs, a new generation of photographers. Because it does help, when you see someone doing something you want to be doing. Especially if that person is someone you can relate to. If we can make that happen, then why not. Let's make it happen.

Flipz

He was interviewed on LBC around the time that album came out, and they were trying to stain him. They were asking questions in the hope that he'd fuck up. But he's too clever. You can't pin something on him.

I saw a different side to him when the album came out. He got on with everyone. He could talk to Manny Norte one minute, then Nick Grimshaw, then the BBC *Breakfast* presenters, and charm them all. He's such a humble guy, there's really no reason to dislike him.

He could always speak to any negative comments, or just brush them off. This is where God comes in as well. So many people try to bring him down – certain newspapers, or the police, like the time they kicked down his door – but they'll never succeed. It's down to God.

He's got a lot of people behind him as well. He really cares about his fans, and I think they know it. He does a lot for them. They are his priority.

Fraser

I think 4:44 and *Gang Signs & Prayer* and *Made in the Manor* are similar, in that they delve into the soul of the artist. I can't remember Jay-Z ever being as personal before. It was more bravado and braggadocio, and we were willing to go along with it, because, well, it's Jay-Z! But 4:44 was the first time he was showing his human side. This was the first time he said, 'I was wrong,' or 'I'm scared.' It's a similar thing with Kano's *Made in the Manor*. And Stormzy took it to a whole new level.

I guess in this age of enlightenment, people are used to seeing behind the gloss of the album sleeve, or the cover shoot. There is a truth to what Stormzy's saying on every track. He had to make it for him, first and foremost. And that's maybe why it worked. He wasn't pandering to anyone.

Flipz

I remember there was a moment after 'Shut Up' where Stormzy was getting a lot of negative attention. People were saying, 'OK, so what? You've had your one hit. But what have you done, really? What have you released, apart from *Dreamer's Disease*?' Then he put out *Gang Signs & Prayer* and it went straight to number one. That shut everyone up pretty quickly.

ambition

I'm up now, look at what God's done
Nah real talk, look at what God did
On the main stage runnin round topless
I phone Flipz and I tell him that we got this
This is God's plan, they can never stop this
Like wait right there, could you stop my verse?
You saved this kid and I'm not your first
It's not by blood and it's not by birth
But oh my God what a God I serve.
'Blinded by Your Grace Pt. 2', *Gang Signs & Prayer*

introduction

Jude

After an exceptional few years, the #Merky team is still working hard. They have often said that they have never really had a moment to come together and celebrate what they've achieved. There might have been a pause once *Gang Signs & Prayer* was released, but it was very brief.

There is, I think, a keen awareness that to stop or slow down would be a mistake. The ambition and hunger the team had before the album came out is still there. They understand that the only way to continue to grow is to keep pushing themselves. 'There's no time to pause,' Tobe says. Rachel spoke about how being uncomfortable is normal, and necessary. Growing pains are essential.

There was, though, plenty to celebrate. Despite last-minute doubts, *Gang Signs & Prayer* went straight in at number one, setting British streaming records in the process. In the album's first week of release, it was certified silver, with seven tracks in the UK Top 40, and all sixteen appearing in the top 100. In 2017 it was nominated for the prestigious Mercury Prize and won Best Album at the MOBO Awards; in 2018 it won the Ivor Novello Award for best album, and Album of the Year at the Brits, as well as winning many other awards and prizes.

Stormzy had become a star. One of very few black

superstars in the UK. But stardom did not come without costs. What's often left out of narratives of success are the inevitable struggles. It's difficult to complain, Stormzy says, but you can imagine what it must be like to live with constant scrutiny, multiple misrepresentations, and a steady stream of hostility. Even now, Stormzy acknowledges that it's easy to dismiss him. What's so surprising, and so inspiring, is Stormzy and the team's refusal to be beaten down by the negativity, and their determination to stay 'normal'. One of the most telling moments in the interviews for me was when Stormzy described parking his car near his house and chatting to a boy who'd run over to say hello. He never wants to feel like that sort of thing couldn't happen, he said. For me, and for those who appreciate his music, it stands as further confirmation of his realness, and his recognition of the people who have taken him to where he is now. Stormzy is a genuine guy, and a nice guy, which is all the more surprising coming from where we both come from. Being cold is not only wise in ends, it's also the inevitable result of living in a place where there is so little hope.

There is a real difficulty in narrating an incomplete journey. Despite the team's ambitions, it's clear that they have not yet been realised, by any means. This is only the first step in what will be a long journey. But it stands as evidence of what can be achieved with foresight, determination and a clean heart.

#Merky are front-runners. Everyone is watching them, hoping to have a similar level of impact. A similar level of unity, and a similar level of success. During the time it's taken to piece together this book, over the summer of 2018 alone, they have put on the sell-out #Merky Festival in Ibiza, brought a walk-out stage into Wireless Festival for the first time, flown hundreds of friends, family and fans out to Menorca for a birthday celebration, announced the #Merky Books publishing imprint and the #Merky scholarship with the University of Cambridge – all at a time when Stormzy himself is working non-stop on a new album. The joke is they have barely started.

There is something undeniable about the past four or five years, and what the team have achieved. It's something that can never be taken away, and something that will live on, both within the pages of this book and within Stormzy's music, as a model for others to follow. Rise up.

10.

Stormzy

I'm so happy that I'm getting to this stage in my career. *Gang Signs & Prayer* was a big moment. It wasn't like a weight off my shoulders, because that makes it sound like a burden. It was more like a stamp in the ground. It was me saying, 'There, now you know.' I wanted it to set the record straight. I wanted it to back up all those people over the years who had said, 'Stormzy's cold, you know. You just don't know how cold he is.' I wanted it to show the world that this is me. It was only after recording the album that I felt like I belonged. Before that, I knew I could make music that's just as good as anyone else, but it was only when I finished it that I felt like I could say I belonged. I spent ten months in the studio, working every hour, and not knowing if it was going to pay off. Are people going to like this? Or are they going to say, 'Oh, dickhead. What's he trying?'

If you're a bad boy at what you do, you deserve success. That's been my whole approach to music. I am 100 per cent sure that I'm a world-class artist. I've always had a mad point to prove, because getting that respect as a black musician in this country is not easy. Where's our Kanye? Where's our Kendrick? Where's our Prince? It's not to say we need that, but where is the spectrum of talented black British musicians who can really stand up against the rest of the world?

I felt like *Gang Signs & Prayer* proved it. Bruv, I'm a musician. I'm a good fucking musician. And if it wasn't enough to prove it, then we go twice as hard for the second album. I just want people to be able to look back on my career and say, 'Yes, he can stand up there with the greats.'

Ayesha

His ambition is to create a legacy, to leave a mark in history. Their vision is to build a team that can grow with them. He doesn't think about him and what's going on in his life, he'll think about the team and what they can achieve.

You only come across a few acts that stand the test of time. For most artists you have a brief period of popularity or notoriety – two or three years at most. But some artists remain. Stormzy has something different something that can endure.

Fraser

Stormzy didn't invent grime, but he perfected it.

Craig David came out of the garage scene in the same way

Stormzy has come out of the grime scene. Craig took what was a very London-centric, home-grown art form to the next level. *Born to Do It* is an album that recognises and references its garage roots. And this is an album that sold a million copies in the US. And Stormzy hits the sweet spot in terms of knowing what it takes to succeed – making incredible art, but also going out there and selling it. I think you have to understand the game, and play the game. It's a very small sweet spot, but he manages to hit it.

You also have to change it up. It's difficult to second-guess what people want. You're never going to keep progressing unless you change it up.

Stormzy

The next stage was touring it. I knew I could be a particular person in the studio, but could I be that person on stage? Would I be able to carry it forward? I remember when I first started playing 'Cigarettes & Cush' and 'Blinded by Your Grace' and I could tell people were a bit confused. At the beginning, anyway.

Trevor

The biggest changes came with *Gang Signs & Prayer*. He'd put so much into the album, but really hadn't given much thought to the tour. His mindset was just, well, we'll go and do what we've got to do. *GSAP* was the first moment when it felt like everything started coming together. Where you could see the power behind it. At that point he could put something out and you could see the impact immediately.

I had to impress upon them the need to plan and do things properly. This is a big step up. This is where we need to go. Tobe got it. At first I had to convince them to bring in my production team. We need lighting. We need visuals. We need to establish a set list. We started to establish the touring team: Kaylum, Stormzy, TiiNY, Flipz, Bronski and Raph.

I said, 'Well, let's sit down and work out a set list, and you can have a look and see what you think.' We put in tracks like 'Blinded by Your Grace', 'Cigarettes & Cush' and '21 Gun Salute', and he was unsure. He couldn't see how they would work live, or if the audience would even want to hear them. So I said, 'Just trust me. Let's try the first show at least and see what happens. We can always make changes afterwards.'

The first show was in Dublin, and I remember standing at the side of the stage when he played '21 Gun Salute'. The whole crowd was singing it back to him. He looked over at me, laughing. I was like, 'See? I told you!'

The tour was sorted, but we decided to ramp it up for the London shows. I said, 'This should be your statement show. People need to remember this.' And he got it. For the first time, his mindset really changed. For a long time I know that when he saw my name on his phone he'd think: Nah, I'm not chatting to Trev. But something changed at Brixton. We had a run-through with a stand-in, so he could see how it worked. And it was amazing. I was walking him around, introducing him to everyone: 'This is your sound guy, this is your lighting guy, this is your visuals guy. This is how we're putting it together.' He got it. He hugged me! I said, 'You're ready to be an artist. Trust me.'

The performance levels are world class. His mindset is, if Jay-Z has performed on the same stage, our performance has to be at his level, at least. He says, 'Trev, just tell me what needs to be done.' We do not play about. We have to be the best.

I remember when Beyoncé performed at Coachella, I just started watching my phone. I knew I'd get a call at some point. Sure enough, when it ended, it started ringing. I didn't even have to look. 'Bruv! Bruv! That was mad! We're going to have to up our game!'

It was mad. It was a statement. Based on the Brixton shows, he got bumped up the order at V Festival, almost immediately. He got bumped up the order at Glastonbury. It was important. He went from being a grime artist to just being an artist.

Stormzy

I take showtime seriously. If we're about to go on tour, or have a festival slot coming up, I'll phone Trev a couple of weeks before, and say, 'Trev.' And he'll just start busting up. Then he'll say, 'Talk to me. What are you thinking?' It's a moving machine. I'm just trying to make everything as good as it can possibly be. Man is trying to give you excellence on every level. Excellence is a universal thing. Excellence can't be denied. And man's an excellent young black boy. I'm very important. That's how I feel. Being an excellent young black boy today, in this world, is defying the odds. I think excellence is something to strive for. I want to make my friends proud, and I want to make my family proud. And I know I can do that, if I'm excellent.

Trevor

With the Brit Awards you have to do a full dress rehearsal and a full camera rehearsal. But Stormzy completely changed it for the final performance. No one had heard it. That was in his heart. I remember he said to me, 'Trev, I'm going to do something a bit different. It's probably better you don't know.' I was like, 'Do what you've got to do, bruv.' He had the message, and he had the platform. You had the whole of the UK watching the Brit Awards.

He'll speak to what matters to him, but he refuses to be manipulated by anyone. So at one show, for example, a politician came along with his family. It was great to have them there, and we really appreciated the support. But at the end of the show, the manager of the venue came up to me and said that this politician was asking if his family could get a picture with Stormzy. What are you going to say? So I took them backstage, and I remember when we walked in, Stormzy just gave me a look. We've got to the stage now where we don't really need to talk sometimes. I knew what he was saying. But the idea was for the kids to get a picture, so I thought it would be calm. When it came time to take the picture, the politician moved forward, so I just had to say, 'No. Just the kids, not you.' He looked at me, and his assistant looked at me, as if to say: How dare you say no! I was like, 'Oh, what, you thought this was some kind of a joke?' I'm happy to be awkward. My priority is Stormzy.

Flipz

Every award he's got he deserves.

I remember he was so nervous at the Brits. We got there, and he couldn't sit still. He was super nervous. We were backstage for a while, and he was just running around, speaking to different people, he couldn't sit still.

I thought he might win one award, but never two. It was Album of the Year that really meant something to him. When he won Best Male we all went mad, but the album award was something else. Before they announced it, he was just sitting there, absolutely still. He really, really wanted it. And when he got it, well, you can see what it meant to him when you watch the video. No disrespect to everyone else who was nominated, but he deserved it. No one worked as hard as him. We were all so happy, because he was so happy.

Fraser

To see Stormzy on stage performing at the Brits, with his top off and the water raining down, was another big moment. It was mind-blowing. He'd talked to me about it eight months before. He'd been planning the Brits performance for a while. And he'd predicted what would happen as well. He said that Album of the Year would be between him and Ed Sheeran, which was quite tongue-in-cheek, but it became a reality. It was the most surreal experience seeing Stormzy performing, just after he'd won and no one had heard the content of his rap except Manon and me before that night. Not even anyone in rehearsals. So to hear the lines about Grenfell and politics booming out to such a huge audience blew me away. It was truly iconic and testament to Stormzy that he used his platform that night to try and do some good in the world.

This performance gave Stormzy a whole new audience. You can tell an artist has broken through when you've got family members from all over the country, who would never know a grime tune, congratulating you.

Trevor

We used to struggle to do what we wanted to do. I'd have quite a few ideas and sound them out with venues, and the response was always the same: 'You can't do this. You definitely can't do that.' Now it's a case of 'How can we help you? What do you need?'

For the Wireless show, for example, we wanted to construct a thrust, so the stage extended out into the crowd. Wireless said no at first: 'Absolutely not. It's physically impossible. You can't do it.' I said, 'You don't understand – this needs to happen.' And so they made it happen. They had to go back to the local authorities, who were arguing that it was unsafe, and wouldn't work for various health and safety reasons, but in the end they got it agreed. Wireless backed us. It paid off.

I got quite a few emails from them afterwards saying how good it was, and how much they enjoyed working with the team. Not to big myself up too much, but it was the first time I saw anyone on social media really commenting on the production itself. And this was due to Tobe's foresight and what he wanted for his artist, Stormzy's attitude of always wanting to push the levels so high, and my amazing core team of Bronski, Amber and Raph. We just wanted to do our best and keep pushing. Investing in your show builds for the future. When you get certain slots, you have to make a statement. Don't just think you can turn up and do your thing. If you pocket the money, you remain static. If you invest in what you're doing, you up the stakes. Look at Wireless. People in the crowd were crying! That's all you can ask for, really. This is why we do what we do. We've proved ourselves. We're not on this earth to settle. We're on this earth to grow and improve. Now if anyone hears Stormzy's name, it's all fine. Anything is possible.

Flipz

Now Stormzy's got his mark in the game. He can go away for a year and come back, because he's made his name. He can build the brand, which is what we've always planned to do.

There are certain doors that Giggs and Wiley kicked down that have allowed Stormzy to do what he does. And now Stormzy's kicked down a massive door. We were always told you can't be from the ends and be commercially successful, and we've proved that you can.

Fraser

This era is such a golden time for musicians, I think. God willing, it will continue for a long time. Artists are able to come through, make the records they want to make, and see commercial and critical success. Stormzy's getting played on the radio not because he's making music that fits a particular mould, but because he's influential. *Gang Signs & Prayer* was a number-one record without any major label push; it was voted for by the people. Stormz was driven by his desire to make something great, and something that he loved. Winning Best Album at the Brits was for me a zenith point of achievement. I feel that to be a part of this rise is the most incredible thing. It's been the most exciting period of my career ever, no doubt. And Stormzy's public acknowledgement of the work that Manon and I put in was incredibly touching. This time – starting with *Made in the Manor* and onwards, and working with visionaries like Kano and Stormzy and Dave – is the best period ever. These are special people. They are not just churned out. That's why we're so lucky to have artists like this creating music at the same time.

Trevor

You could say that the whole scene is changing, because of what we've done as a team. Just take the pop-up shows we did around the album launch, for example. We had London on standby.

We're front runners. The whole culture is watching us. And

everyone thinks there's this massive team responsible, but there isn't. We've changed the game. It's heavy, and it's hard. For Wireless alone, it took a lot to put it all together. A lot of sleepless nights. Over a hundred people working together to make it happen. But it was worth it.

So much work went into it. Take for example the visual we created for 'Return of the Rucksack', the one of Stormzy's head carved out of stone, and cracked. So for that I had to take a 3D photograph of his head. I called him up and said, 'Listen, I need you for an hour. There's a car coming to pick you up.' The car collected him and brought him to this little backstreet studio where we had a chair set up with hundreds of cameras positioned around it. At first he was like, 'What is this?' But when he saw the results, he was amazed. He could see what we were doing.

Stormzy's driven, and he wants to be the best. Tobe's the same. Akua's the same. The whole team is the same. Everyone is passionate about what they do. It's not about money. We love what we do. And we're doing it for all the right reasons. We're making noise, and we're making it in the right way. We're winners. You can't tell us otherwise.

We're not doing it to show off, or to compete. We're not here to compete against other artists. We're just here to put out amazing work and try and raise the bar for the whole scene.

And we don't rest on our laurels. No one settles. Everyone pushes each other. There's always more to do.

Akua

I think what Stormzy was really trying to say with *Gang Signs & Prayer* was that he is an artist. He was trying to show people that his range is much wider than what you think it is. His ambitions are much bigger than what you think they might be. So with R&B, gospel and rap, he's letting you know: 'I'm capable of so much more than you think.' And that's what we do in everything. We don't do what you think would be the norm or the standard. We always try and exceed it.

It's going to be the same going forward. You just can't pigeonhole him. That's a problem in the industry, and with the media. They want to put you in a box. And they don't know what to do with you if you don't fit in that box. There's always a reason for those boxes, but they only serve the people who put you in them.

11.

Stormzy

I'm confident, and I back myself, but that doesn't mean that I don't have doubts. I can say, 'I'm going to play Wembley,' but that doesn't mean I don't sit at home and worry about how I'm going to do it.

I wasn't really ready for it all. Take the Channel 4 interview, which was really supposed to be about the album. But they asked me a question about depression, and I answered it, and that became the focus. Don't get it twisted – I'm happy with my answer, and I'm happy with the message I helped to spread, but I *hated* it at the time. I had real problems with it. I mean, I don't know how to cope with mental health problems. I just turn my phone off and don't speak to anyone. I can't be an ambassador. And then NME put my photo on the front cover, so all of a sudden I'm a poster boy for depression.

A similar thing happened with the time the police kicked my door in. I didn't want it to blow up the way it did. I was being naive. Again, it was good to remind everyone that racism is alive, and that the feds are still kicking down doors, but that's not what I wanted.

A lot of the time, I can't lie, I'm happy to be all the things that people say I am, and I feel like I am and that I'm meant to be. Leader, brother, boyfriend, role model, political commentator, advocate for mental health and whatnot. But a lot of the time I don't. I'm just a musician. That's all I can really concentrate on. I'm proud of what I've achieved, and I want these things, but I don't think I'm strong enough to be these things. I don't think I'm old enough to be these things. Some days I don't want to be a role model, because some days I'm not a role model. I can see why people might want me to be a particular person. I'm blessed, but I'm human.

This is why we follow God, because humans are flawed. People will say, 'Yeah, but you stepped up for the role.' And all right, I did, so I take it. But I didn't really sign up for everything.

Rachel

Don't get me wrong, there's a lot of love for him, but there are a lot of people out to get him, a lot of people who are angry. Many tabloids email me regularly asking for comment on pointless stories with the sole aim of dragging him down, and most of the time I simply don't respond. One called me the other day and said, 'We've had an eye witness state that Stormzy was trying to get away from being harassed by some blokes in central London the other evening.' On this particular night, he wasn't actually in London. However, I thought to myself, so what if he was!? If someone's harassing you, most people try and get away from the situation. He's only human . . . Give the guy a break. Let him be normal for just five minutes. And, sadly, the NME situation. The irony in that particular debacle is despite us saying we didn't want to participate, they put him on the cover of their mental health issue – without our permission – and without considering how that cover may make him feel. Yes, he very bravely spoke about his personal struggles with mental health openly on Channel 4, however that wasn't a confirmation for him to be a poster boy for mental health.

I fear many of the public think that because someone's famous, they're unbreakable, they're numb to feeling sad or low. Because they're wealthy, they have everything they need, life is so great, right?! And a lot of the time they couldn't be more wrong. I just wish there was more of an understanding from the outside world on that particular topic. I frequently tell him we as humans weren't built to live the life that he leads.

There will always be journalists and particular publications that are out to get him. However, as you get more relaxed within the public eye, you learn to not sweat the small stuff, and I often say to him – it's just tomorrow's fish and chip paper.

I saw a piece recently which called Stormzy a political pop hero, and he is. Not in the way that he's supporting any particular party, but because he's shining a light on subjects that mean something to him, and that mean something to a lot of people that don't have a platform to raise awareness on. He's a spokesman of black empowerment, social activism and so much more.

Take the Cambridge Scholarship for example. Stormzy didn't just recognise the lack of diversity at these elite universities but he actually did something about it.

I saw many people across social media deeming it racist, which is beyond ignorant. I read something the other day which summed it up: 'The trouble is that many people measure most things based on their own lifecycle and can't understand that history still counts. So when they see black people winning at things like this, they think it's not fair.' And what they don't realise is – in Stormzy's words – the score isn't even close to equalling the game.

Ayesha

When you're black you have to work twice as hard to be noticed. I think that's obvious to everyone of colour. You don't walk down the street and think you've got it the same as everyone else. You know that you have to work even harder to be taken seriously. I wouldn't call it pressure. It's more personal than that.

He's very aware of his ethnicity. I mean, he's Ghanaian, so his mum was never not going to let him be very aware of that fact! He's proud of his background.

Stormzy

I feel in some ways as if I'm from a different era. I'm a social-media kid, but I know that social media can be a bad thing.

It's hard to realise it.

There are some things you're not meant to know. You're not meant to know what some random person thinks about what you're wearing. This is why we have little white lies. This is why we have social niceties. We can't really handle the truth. It's like, if I ask someone, 'What do you think of this outfit?' The worst thing they'll say is, 'I'm not sure. You should maybe try a different top.' They will never say, 'Bro, it's fucking shit. What the fuck are you wearing? Take it off.' All those filters are torn down now.

If I put up a picture, a thousand people might have an opinion. I'm not meant to hear that many thoughts. I'm not meant to wake up and see what any person is on, first thing in the morning. You're not meant to be plugged in to that many people. Without the Internet, you would have your family. You'd have your school friends. You'd have your work friends. They'd never really mix. Before social media, you might have known what your siblings were on, if that. You might have known a bit of hood news, maybe. The Internet breaks down all of those walls.

There are people online who can diss me or my friends, who can say something online, and get everyone to laugh at us. In real life, that person wouldn't say anything. If he's in the room, he wouldn't say anything. Nothing. Online, not only is he going to attack you, he's going to get a thousand people to attack you as well. You can't win. Regardless of what we are doing, the Internet warrior will win. It doesn't matter how much success you have, how many people love you. Reality doesn't matter. He says something stupid, and he wins.

Don't get me wrong, there are so many incredible things

about social media. But I can sometimes go on social media and start to question everything.

In a lot of situations online, the answers are just staring at you. Like, I'll be reading some discussion on Twitter, and I'll think: Wait a second – why are they having an argument about this? If there were ten sane people in a room, this would be over in a second.

Ayesha

I couldn't describe a typical Stormzy fan. Part of what makes Stormzy popular, and what makes Stormzy authentic, is the fact that he is honestly just himself. He has no filter. And there is no one in the background controlling what he does or what he says. That wouldn't be real. He doesn't position himself as a conscious rapper, he just choses to rap. He comes across as honest because he is. And that's what has attracted so many different types of people to him, I think. People of all ages are Stormzy fans. But there are kids who are growing up with Stormzy. The artists I grew up with had such a big impact on my life. And that is the same now with Stormzy, he becomes a part of their life – their memories, their conscience and their growth.

Stormzy

There are lots of ideas that sound great. The reality is very different.

You can say to someone, 'Yeah, bro, I got you!' That's easy. But if that person called you up at 2 a.m., having a crisis of

Dublin and #Merky Festival, Ibiza.

DETTM. Making plans with Akua.

The family, backstage.

The Brit Awards, 2018.

'I got two sisters, one black mum, they raised a prince. Raised up by black girl magic, what did you think?' Brits 2018 performance.

(Clockwise from top left) Tobe and TiiNY. Twin B. Fraser T. Smith. Flipz. Ed Sheeran. Flipz and Kaylum.

Wireless 2018.

Team #Merky.

some sort, are you going to pick up? The reality of really being there for someone is different.

The first challenges we faced are the same challenges we're facing now. Trying to do something that's not been done before is difficult, because there's no obvious way to navigate through it. You've got to work out how to do everything yourself. We're on our own. There are no comparisons for what we're trying to do. There are no models. I'm none of these people. What I'm trying to do, I've not seen anyone do. I haven't seen anyone sit in that space.

Who I'm trying to be, and what I'm trying to create, and what I'm trying to mean to people, and what I'm trying to stand for, is all completely new. No one has done it before. Not by young black brothers coming from where we're coming from, and spitting what we're spitting. I wanted to make 'Big for Your Boots' and 'Blinded by Your Grace, Pt. 2'. I wanted to be that guy.

If you want to be something great, you have to realise that you will have to put in the work, and you have to be prepared for hardships. It's not easy. I've had people discredit my character and my music, not because of my character or my music, but because of who I am.

I accept there are some people who are just not going to like my music. That's fine. I respect people who don't like it. But I can't get along with the fact that people attack me just because of what I'm doing.

I'm very understanding of the time we're in, and of what comes with it. I knew it came with the territory. You can't aim to be who I'm trying to be and not expect a level of resistance.

Akua

I want to just live my life in my own lane. That's why I could never be famous. I want the space and the freedom to make mistakes and learn from them. That's the thing about social media – it encourages people to think that everything is their business, and it isn't.

That's why we own our narratives and try to tell our story as much as possible because otherwise it will just get distorted.

Most of the time we don't comment. We just leave it. Newspapers will run pieces that are nonsense. It's like the story that Stormzy was demanding a certain amount of money to appear at Labour Live. There was no conversation about that whatsoever. Why would Stormzy headline a political rally? I don't know where the story came from, but it appeared. And so what can you do? You can't sweat it.

One of the things we always talk about is how to empower people. Stormzy himself is a bit of an anomaly, but the ambition or the desire to create is not an anomaly. Everyone has the capability to create. If we have things that he's passionate about, that he can translate into projects – we can make an opening, or crack open the door, so people can find it and move through. And so much of it is outside of music. Sometimes he's more excited about things outside of music than music itself.

I don't understand why people compare music. People don't think about what musicians might put into their work. You might wake up in the morning and have an argument with your girlfriend and that might be the basis for your biggest hit. It doesn't mean that if I now write a song about an argument they'll sound the same, or that they're even worthy of comparison. Let people enjoy things! Not everything is a competition. It's especially a problem within the black music space. People always try and pitch people against each other. It's always a competition. There's always beef. It's always the same.

It's also about not watching what anyone else is doing. If you're going into the studio to make an album, and worrying about albums that other people have made, then you're already off base. You're putting yourself on the back foot. It's so restrictive. Why not give yourself the freedom of creativity and expression?

Stormzy

I've had to deal with racism for a long time. I can't control who listens to my music. I've had racist lads commenting from time to time. I'm going to get the problematic parody videos. I'm going to get the neeky renditions, or the neeky politicians or television personalities standing up and using my words. People are entitled to their opinions, of course. People can take what I say and claim it in some way, and I can call shit out, but I can't control how my words are used, or what people take from my music. There are some serious issues here, but I think that what I'm doing is so new, it's going to take a bit of time for the general public to get used to it.

Take 'Shut Up'. I remember so clearly the first day, the first week, the first month after it came out. That was the authentic, raw sound. It's a Ruff Sqwad riddim, but it's raw. It's a bad-boy freestyle. Music is a thing you give to the world, and that's all you can do. That's my only job. I just have to make sure it's excellent. People can talk shit, but I know what it is.

People were telling me that grime was dead when *Gang Signs & Prayer* came out. Is it? Is 'Big for Your Boots' not grime? Why is it not grime? Why? Listen to the lyrics:

> Wanna come round here like a bad boy? Do it
>> Bun all the talking, go on then, do it
>> Running through the party, bottle of Bacardi
>> Bro's in my ear saying 'Stormz, don't do it'
>> Devil on my shoulder, I don't lack
>> Hit 'em with a crowbar, I don't scrap
>> Even when I'm sober, I'm so gassed
> Say you ride but there's no car and no mash.

Why is that not grime?

At the end of the day, fame comes with some nonsense. It can feel vicious, and overwhelming, but let's be real, it's not the worst thing that I could be dealing with, is it. It's not bad compared to what most people deal with.

I know who I am. I can't get twanged. I know I'm good.

It's always been a beautifully confusing thing when I find myself being praised for certain things I've done or I've achieved. This is gonna sound like I'm trying to be humble or trying to sound like the ultimate nice guy so let me be wary of how I word this. But take the Brits performance for example. I was quite famous before, and God willing, I'm still gonna be successful afterwards. All I did was dedicate two bars to Grenfell. I sat down and wrote something out. And yeah of course it's very dismissive to reduce that whole gesture to just writing a couple of bars, of course it is. But in terms of what's actually happened, in terms of the people who lost their lives and the people who are still suffering, and the fact that the government has tried to sleep on a tragedy, it's nothing. There's no suffering.

As a young black man coming from the community that I come from, I recognise that I have responsibilities. If I'm going to be on stage for five minutes at the Brit Awards, I have a responsibility. Bearing in mind that not one of us has been on that stage for a very long time, if it's ever happened. If I have five minutes, I've got to use that time wisely.

We live in this world. We know that racism exists. It's getting better, maybe, but it still exists. We know that we have to work twice as hard to get anywhere. So when one of us succeeds, we have a responsibility.

I'm not trying to be that corny don. I'm not on some presidential shit. I just know that no one is going to help my little brother. You can talk about things, but you have to take action. Man can go on stage and spray a two-bar about the prime minister and get a reaction. But there's a lot more I can do. It's a duty.

DJ TiiNY

Everyone is entitled to their own opinion. This is real life, and everyone's human. People say what they say, and you can choose what to listen to. I choose not to listen to the negative. Tobe schooled me: pay no attention to them.

Stormzy deep down is a good person. Growing up in London is hard and everyone's got to do what they've got to do. I don't think you can criticise that. It's not easy being Stormzy. He's trying to do something with his life. Not many people from the ends are trying to do what he's doing. It takes courage to go and do what he's doing.

Stormzy

There's a problem with the visibility of black British culture in our country. It's only now that black Britishness has a chance to really exist. I was walking down the street the other day with my bredrin, someone who hadn't really been out in public with me that much. And he said, 'Rah! Everyone's clocking you.' I said, 'Bruv, do you know why it is? Which black people did you see on the telly? Me, Idris Elba, John Boyega, and maybe Tinie Tempah, a little bit further back.' If people see a big black man walking down the street, of course they'll know it's me. There's only a few of us on the telly. We're still learning as we go along.

The thing is, I know man's sick. I've always known. Man's ready to sit on the sofa with Jonathan Ross. Man's ready to go on the Brit Awards and spit my black lyric and play my black music and talk about who I am and what I do. I know it's sick. I know it's marketable. People tell me we're sick. So why can't we show the country that we're sick? Why can't we show the world? Is it just because they might not get it? OK, they might not get the lyrics, they might not get the sound, they might not get the culture. But if it's sick, they *should* get it. There's a lot of things that I like that I don't really have much knowledge of. But I learn about it. I get it.

Black British culture is sick. Just get me on the radio. Get me on the telly. I'll show everyone.

There are some big differences between the UK and the US. We've each got our own problems. But black culture is the prevalent culture in the US, without question. And for some reason, black culture is still alien to the UK.

Akua

Being conscious and just wanting to do your own thing are not mutually exclusive. What the world perceives as being conscious, and what you just want to do, can exist together. And that's the space in which we exist. You don't have to watch what anyone else is doing to determine your decisions. You can wake up in the morning and want to do something for young people and you can. You don't have to follow the woke agenda. You can care about black people without going to marches. You can care about young black boys without writing essays on Instagram about knife crime or gun crime. The world wants to tell you the way to respond to social issues.

But you've got to do it your own way. You don't have to tell everyone.

There's a lot of sheep. There's a move towards a collective mentality. People are driven by perception. I've never been like that. And neither has Stormzy. So you might not like books, but he does. So he can speak about his love for poetry or literature and it will resonate with people who feel similarly.

If you're someone who is spiritual or who believes in God, you'll know that all of the showboating is for nothing anyway. Everything you do is between you and God. The difference is that Stormzy has a platform. And if he has an idea that he thinks can make a difference, or help or empower people, he can use that platform. But that's not so that we can tick any boxes for anybody. We just have our ideas and we get on with it.

Everyone has their own individual reasons for why they do or they don't care about particular things. So, you might care about knife crime because you might know someone who has been a victim of it. I might be watching the news and just think young black men need something – mentoring or better opportunities. It's a completely different perspective but I still have the same compassion and care.

Stormzy

I think our relationship with stardom within the black British community is changing. In this country, we're not really used to superstardom. We've been used to artists going through the motions and then disappearing. Or a kind of distasteful superstardom, where the artist just rubs everyone up the wrong way. As much as I might be a star, I realise I'm only a star in my music, in my shows, in my campaigns. I'm not a star as a person. I'm still Mike. The biggest Stormzy fan might bump into me on the street and for the first minute or two they might treat me like a star. But if they talk to me, they'll quickly realise I'm just a person. I'm someone they might get along with or might not get along with. That's really important to me. I never want to be anyone other than Mike.

Don't get it twisted. I know that fame changes things, but I try to stop it from changing too much. A normal day for me is wake up, have some breakfast, maybe bun a zoot, drive over to the studio, have a chat with whoever is there, record something, walk down to the shops, come back. There's no shield of celebrity, if that's a way to describe it. I've tried to avoid that shield as much as possible. Sometimes you can't avoid it, but I don't like it.

That's why I'm wary of being seen as someone who wants to teach people. Just because I've enjoyed some success doesn't mean that people should listen to me above anyone else. I'm not about to say, 'Come on, guys, put the knives down.' On that particular subject, I can only speak about what I've experienced, which isn't a lot. I can guess what it's like today, but I can only speak to what I know. There's no way someone like me could pretend to have the answers, or that anyone would pay attention if I stood up and said, 'You need to listen to me.' I don't ever want to be the person way over here, talking about what's happening over there.

Over the years I've somehow become this commentator. On Twitter or Instagram, if I say something, I always try and add in a disclaimer, because what do I know? I'm just a man of my heart. I can see something on the news, and it can move me or make me think, and I'll talk about it from that point of view. That's the only way I can speak to it. I recognise that I have a platform, and that I'm lucky enough to have fans who listen to what I say, but I'm just speaking for myself. There's no real difference between me and anybody else. I know who I am.

It's like, I was round my best friend's house the other day. His family home is in Thornton Heath, and his family is my family so I always pop round for a catch up or to just chill. They recently had some German exchange students staying with them, who were about thirteen or fourteen years old, and I walked in and the exchange students were gobsmacked. They turned out to be big fans. It was that crazy paradox of being with friends and family who still just see me as Mike, until something happens that quickly reminds us that a lot has changed. That's a good indication of what my life's like at the moment.

Rachel

I strongly believe you have to find comfort in discomfort. It's similar to growing pains. Being uncomfortable hurts, but you're growing. We've definitely had some turbulent times but we live and we definitely learn, and nine out of ten times it always comes full circle.

Stormzy

I'm still the underdog in so many respects. I might be a headline act at Wireless, but I'm one of three headline acts, and it's safe to say that I'm the smallest of the three. People are there to see people other than me. I'm also easy to dismiss: I'm mainstream, which for whatever reason can sometimes be deemed as not being for the culture. I don't agree. I'm grateful for the culture that inspired me and has allowed me to flourish, and I'm trying to expand it and move it forward.

I don't understand people who feel the need to criticise new music. Don't be negative. Let black British music thrive. It just needs space to exist. It's never been allowed to exist like this. And now it does, let it be. Don't get it twisted – discussions are healthy. But no one cares what we think. This is why I love music. I could be sitting here commenting on some artist, and meanwhile, that artist is in an arena somewhere right now shelling down in front of 25,000 people who love him and don't care what we think.

When all is said and done, it's undeniable. You can listen to all the conversations, but music is undeniable. People can talk shit, but the music exists.

Ayesha

'Potential' for me is a negative word. It's an abstract concept. There's no end point.

He takes his time. He won't be rushed. He won't put anything out unless he really believes in it. He's so particular with his craft. Like, he'll finish a track, and we'll go back and listen to it, and he'll say, 'Nah, I need to chop it up and do it again.'

12.

Alec (Twin)

I knew that Stormzy had it in him to become that big. I'm glad I was right, for his and the music's sake. It was never a label thing. I thought he was a very important artist and person, and just needed to progress in his own way, and with the right type of expertise at the right time.

His intentions were always good. I found his reasons for doing music so respectable and commendable. I really bought in to that. And as I am a Christian and of faith, I respected how much his faith mattered to him. I think he knew my intentions were pure. He knew I just wanted the best for him.

Stormzy

I'm not sure about the word 'humble'. It might be humility for some people, but for me, it's always about the art. Take 'Bad Boys', for example. People say, 'Oh, you should have gone last,

Ghetts has the coldest verse,' but it wasn't right for the song. I don't care about where people come or how things might be perceived if it doesn't work. Ghetts was always meant to go at the end. That's the only way it would work. My whole philosophy is the best idea wins. That's it.

With the next album, the challenge will be trying to keep all of the elements that I know people love, but also moving everything forward. Because there's a duty to keep it original, and keep it real, and stick to where you come from. That's all well and good, but I can't act like I'm in the same situation I was when I was twenty. I'm not living that life any more. Things are not the same. As I see it, my duty is to talk about my life as it is: where I come from, where I'm at now, what's good and what's shit, what I enjoy and what I miss. What else can I talk about? *Gang Signs & Prayer* was all of those things, so the next album has to be about all of those things, too.

When I first got in the studio, I was feeling the music, but there was a lot missing. Where's the 'Blinded by Your Grace'? Where's the '100 Bags'? It's not about me trying to be someone else, it's me being who I am today. What am I doing? What do I stand for? What am I trying to learn and figure out for myself? My duty is to figure that out. It's got to be Stormzy today. These are the facts of the matter.

I've got to be confident. If you're scared of your truth, then you have no reason to be confident. But I'm not scared of my truth. If you tell the truth, the whole truth, and nothing but the truth, you'll be all right. Someone once asked me why *Gang Signs & Prayer* was so short. It was a bit of a strange question, because length was never a consideration when I made it. You'd never think: Oh, it's got to be fifteen songs. It's that length because that's how long it took me to say everything I wanted to say. There was nothing I left out.

Fraser

Stormzy can't play it safe on the next record. He just has to go deeper. Some of the tracks on *Gang Signs & Prayer* were cliffhangers, as well. It's like with 'Lay Me Bare'. Does the story end there? He's got to scratch that itch, and go and meet and talk to his dad. I also want people to acknowledge him as a bona fide singer, not just as a rapper who sings. I think the grime tracks have to be even harder, and the beautiful tracks have to be even more beautiful. A lot has happened since the first album, don't forget. Success brings huge change, good and bad. That's the yin and yang of life. There have been incredible highs, but also incredible lows. Personal and social responsibility now weighs on his young shoulders. But he's strong, resilient. I know he's going to be around for a very long time, and will be looked back on as someone who not only changed music, but who did so much good in the world too.

Stormzy

I want to express my confidence with the next album. I'm learning I can express myself in different ways. It's about the riddim. It's about my flow. It's about how I'm sitting on that riddim. I learned that from Jay-z. 'I figure I'm Jigga' – just those four words are so cold. Or H.E.R. and 'Focus'. Just the way she says 'Me' at the beginning. It's such a lazy flow, but it's so confident. There's excellence in simplicity sometimes.

The next album will be everything that's happened to me since I made Gang Signs & Prayer. And everything I didn't talk about on Gang Signs & Prayer. And everything that has changed in my life, because a lot has changed. It's me being more vulnerable, more confident, more honest, more cut-throat, more direct, more assertive. It's not going to be the same as GSAP. As long as it's excellent, it's a foolproof plan.

Kaylum

I'm not doing what I do to win awards. I'm doing what I do because I love it.

I'm so busy now. It's mad. I don't see my family much. But I have this thing – work first. I would rather take every opportunity, and do everything I can do now. Might as well rake it in. I'm only twenty. There's no time for normality. There will be – but not now.

These opportunities don't come along all the time, so when they do, you have to say yes. I like working. I don't like not working. I'd like to be more busy, really and truly.

I've just started a production company with GRM. I mean, I don't take bookings at the moment. I don't really have time to keep up with my emails. I was talking to Posty at GRM, and just thought: Why not set up something with them? Is there a way to create videos for young up-and-coming artists using the best young up-and-coming videographers? So we did. The videos are cheap and quick and high quality. And the videographers are looked after – we buy the equipment and put them on a wage so they're comfy, and have them shoot all the videos.

Stormzy

I've also been lucky enough to meet quite a few of my heroes. It can be a nice, normal conversation, most of the time because they don't know who I am. Or they have wisdom to impart. I just try and go with the flow, and try and learn as much as possible. I try and figure out their approach to life, or their steez, if you know what I mean. I met someone recently who was just a legendary figure. And you could tell, instantly. With that level of experience and success comes a level of class, and composure, and calmness, that I would love to try and adopt. He knew who he was. He didn't need to try and please anyone. I saw him rehearse, and he was just chatting during the soundcheck, just talking about his life. He was just being him. And I felt that there's something I need to take on board. I've just got to be Stormzy. Don't ever let these fools make you think that you can't do 'Blinded by Your Grace, Pt. 1'!

Tobe

Stormzy has sort of gone beyond our scene, now. It's new territory for us – we're having to learn a lot, but we're also trying to share that knowledge. Like, we have to make sure producers register with ASCAP, the American Society of Composers, Authors and Publishers, so they can receive royalties from US sales, and so they can be eligible for US awards. It's not something that's come up before, because we didn't really think it could be possible before. Like, there's been a generation of artists that have opened the doors for us in the US in many ways, but trying to win a Grammy isn't really an ambition for a lot of UK artists, and it should be. I just thought: Why not? It's a confidence thing, maybe. I'm not saying we're going to win one, but why not try? Why can't we chase it? It's got to become the norm, you know.

Stormzy is never going to leave people behind. If he's going for the Grammys he wants everyone to go for the Grammys. He's also going to work with the producers and engineers he likes. It's not a case of moving on to work with people with more experience, it's like, let's just work to get to that standard.

Stormzy

History is important.

I realise I'm the most blessed, in terms of a young British rapper getting opportunities and being listened to. I realise I'm blessed.

There was man clashing in the playground. There was the 168 mixtape. There are all of these things. I go back to that mixtape, and listen to Thea's intro, and just realise how long the journey has been.

Flipz

I've been at the studio when he's recorded most things. At first I was just there as his bredrin. Just watching. But if you're there as much as I was there, you'll learn. You'll always learn something when you're in the studio with Stormzy. I've watched him grow as an artist. Even down to his pen game, and how he writes.

He's a good guy, and he's a smart guy, and he knows what he wants. And he puts that energy and ambition into all of us. It might not be in a nice way sometimes, but we know what he's trying to do. We know what he's trying to achieve, we can see the bigger picture.

Trevor

People on the outside are really starting to buy in to the #Merky brand now. Take the #Merky Festival for example. Last year it was one day, and it was a lot of fun. This year it was two days, and it sold out immediately.

I've got my own company, but #Merky is something else. It's a family.

One of the main things about #Merky is that we all think the same way. We all have our own individual roles, but we know what the bigger task is. It's quite funny, because there are a lot of people we work with who know us each individually, and will get an answer they don't like from one of us and take the question to someone else. I mean, what do they think the answer will be?

Earlier this year, I was asked if I could become a tour manager for an artist, who I won't name. I had a few meetings about it. They even flew me out to New York. This artist is major. What they were discussing was a worldwide stadium tour, for a year and a half. And they basically said, 'Name your price.' The money would have set me up for a very long time. It was mad.

It was also a chance to do something different. I don't want our company to just be known for working with urban artists. We also have classical artists, gospel artists. I think taking this job would have broken every possible ceiling. It would have taken the company to a whole other level. So from a financial point of view, and a professional point of view, it was a good idea. But it had to be me. We're talking about managing 250 people, on shows around the world. I would have no time for anything else. I spoke to Tobe about it, and he couldn't believe it. He said, 'Trev, don't worry. I understand.'

A couple of days later I was talking to my other half about it, and she just said, 'Your heart's not in it, is it?' And she was right. This tour would have been huge, but it would have all been handed to me. It would sell out in seconds. It was just a job. Whereas with Stormzy, and with #Merky, I've grown with it. I've helped to build it. We've done it all together. The rewards are so different. You can't beat what we've done. It's history.

I couldn't imagine not being there to help out with his future tours. I've done everything so far, from local shows to overseas tour to Glastonbury to his first headline shows. How could I not be there?

Stormzy

I want #Merky to be a hub of endless possibilities. #Merky Records is one thing. But #Merky could be anything. It could be a hospital, or a school, or a manufacturing company, or a colour. A #Merky black. Do you get what I mean? I don't know what the next thing will be, but when I hear it, I know it. This is where my self-confidence comes in.

Ayesha

It's authentic. Tobe and Stormz have a good eye. They know what will work for them, and what won't.

It happened instantly. Although we're all very different, and had different upbringings, and grew up in different areas, we all understand each other. We all have our own strengths. And everyone will do anything for one another. Tobe and Stormzy have the final say, but in our team no one is really in charge. Everyone has an opinion, and everyone is allowed an opinion.

Tobe always says, 'Don't worry about it. We're God-blessed. God's got us.'

Stormzy

I'm still friends with all the people I was rolling with before I got into music, Mark, Rimes, Konz. Konz was my best friend growing up. But Flipz was making the music with me. He was in the studio every day.

He is my twin. We think the same. We're always on the

same page. We barely clash. The thing is, people banter with Flipz, and say, 'Allow us, we don't live the #Merky way of life.' It's funny, but it's true. We can be in a meeting together, and someone will say something distasteful, and we'll both clock it. It's the same with the team. I know how everyone thinks, and they'll know how I think.

It's more than connectedness. It's like it's in our DNA.

It's really because these people have allowed me to be great. They've allowed me to move how I move, and support me in a way that I'll be forever grateful for.

I'm in a position now where I can make things happen, thank God. I can set up a scholarship that gets young black kids into Cambridge. But that only happens because I've got Akua on my team, and Akua is a genius. I've got Rachel, who's the best publicist in the UK. I just have the ideas. I'm a bit like a kid in that respect. So I had the idea for the scholarship, but they make it happen. If there are any difficult questions I know that they will have the answers. With the Cambridge scholarship thing, Akua organised it all. She made it all happen. All I did was get in the car, eat my food, turn up and say hello, speak to the students, take some pictures, jump in the car and go home. That's it.

Stormzy

Nothing we're doing today shocks us. There's no optimism. We're very pragmatic. If I was to say to Tobe, 'Listen, by 2030 #Merky Enterprises should be a billion-dollar company,' his reaction would be, 'OK, let's make it happen.' When we can see something, and want it to happen, we make it happen. That's the difference.

Tobe

There's no time to pause. We looked at 2018 and thought it might be an all right year, we're going to be calm. But it hasn't happened that way at all.

It's a constant race against myself, almost. I'll never complain about it. Before getting into it this deep, it's always something I aspired to. We've got something big we're working on. There's always something keeping us busy.

Rachel

I guess we don't often take stock and celebrate what we've achieved (although we must!). It's always on to the next thing.

Stormzy

Do you know the biggest challenge I face? It's knowing that at the end of this, I should be exactly who I'm supposed to be. That I have achieved everything I'm supposed to achieve. I have the tools to do that. But I've just got to make it happen. That's my challenge.

And more than anything, I want to be able to look at the fruits of my labour. Not in a self-serving way, but just to see that the work I've done is making a difference in some way. Like, I'd love to be fifty or so, and to be able to go into #Merky Enterprises, and meet a young graduate on an internship, killing it. Or to see a doctor who's come through the Stormzy Scholarship scheme excelling in her field. That would be everything.

It's coming, and not just for me. There's so much to look forward to.

Akua

We're so proud of Stormzy and we all feel a sense of being so blessed to be a part of the team. I remember at the end of Wireless I was so emotional because I just felt: We've come so far, and we've made it to this point. The show was next level. And you think about everything you go through to get here. You're not gassed. You're privileged to be there, and to be working beside him. But everyone is also made to understand what they bring to the table. And that respect is always given.

And then you wake up the next morning and it's back to business as usual.

For more information on #Merky Books, please visit:

www.penguin.co.uk/merkybooks

timeline

2014

20 June: Releases *Not That Deep* EP independently.

20 July: Releases *Dreamer's Disease* EP independently. The EP makes it to #1 in the iTunes Hip-hop/Rap chart.

22 October: Wins Best Grime Act at the MOBO Awards.

Late October: Appears on 'Later with Jools Holland', becoming the first unsigned rapper to do so, performing the song 'Not That Deep'.

November: Collaborates with rappers Chip and Shalo on 'I'm Fine'.

2015

7 January: Comes #3 in the 'BBC Introducing Top 5' on Radio 1.

25 February: Kanye West performs at the Brit Awards and invites an entourage of grime artists onstage, including Stormzy.

8 March: Releases the single 'Know Me From'. The track peaks at #49 in the UK charts, #7 in the UK R&B chart, and #2 in the UK Independent chart.

17 May: Releases 'Shut Up' as a freestyle video on YouTube, a video that has now amassed almost 80 million views.

29 June: Wins the award for Best International Act: UK at the 15th BET Awards.

September: Releases the final instalment of his 'Wicked Skengman' freestyle series onto iTunes, along with a studio version of his 'Shut Up' freestyle. The freestyle series peaks at #18 in the UK charts, the first freestyle to ever break the UK Top 40, and #2 in the UK R&B and Independent charts.

17 September: 'Know Me From' wins the award for Best Video at the Rated Awards, after also being nominated for Best Track, and Stormzy for Artist of the Year.

4 November: Wins the awards for Best Grime and Best Male After at the MOBO Awards, as well as being nominated for Best Video.

12 December: Performs 'Shut Up' during Anthony Joshua's ring-walk for his fight versus Dillian Whyte.

18 December: 'Shut Up' becomes #8 in the UK Singles Chart after a campaign to get it to #1 in time for Christmas is launched. The single goes Platinum and also becomes Stormzy's highest-charting single.

2016

April: Drops single 'Scary'.

5 June: Wins *The Times* Breakthrough Award at the Southbank Sky Arts Awards.

26 June: Nominated for a BET Award, Best International Act: UK.

26 August: Makes his acting debut in the film *Brotherhood*, the third and final instalment in the trilogy of 'Hood' films.

6 September: Wins Artist of the Year at the Rated Awards.

16 September: Wins the Innovator Award at the AIM Independent Music Awards after also being nominated for Independent Breakthrough of the Year.

November: Nominated for two MOBO Awards: Best Male and Best Grime.

2017

15 January: Named by Forbes as one of their 30 Under 30 in Europe for the category 'Entertainment'.

Early February: Returns from his social media hiatus via a series of billboard campaigns across London displaying the hashtag #GSAP 24.02.

3 February: Releases the single 'Big For Your Boots' which peaks at #6 in the UK charts and tops the UK R&B and Independent charts. It goes Platinum in the UK and is his most successful single up to that point.

7 February: Announces a 16-date UK tour for his upcoming album. It sells out in minutes, so he adds another date in Brixton shortly afterwards.

17 February: Announces on Twitter that his brand, #Merky, is 'officially an indie label'.

22 February: Receives a nomination for British Breakthrough Act at the Brits and performs alongside Ed Sheeran at the event.

24 February: *Gang Signs & Prayer* is released, his debut studio album, and he also releases the singles 'Cold' and 'Cigarettes & Kush'. 'Cold' peaks at #2 in the UK R&B and Independent charts.

3 March: *Gang Signs and Prayer* debuts at #1 on the UK Albums Chart and goes Platinum in the UK, becoming the first grime album to hit number one. The album received 69,000 combined chart sales in its first week. Meanwhile, Spotify announce that Stormzy's album broke their 'first-week album streams by a British artist' record, garnering more than 18 million streams.

6 June: Nominated for a Silver Clef Award for Best Live Act.

24 June: Plays a huge set with a high-profile slot on The Other Stage at Glastonbury.

25 June: Wins the BET Award for Best International Act: Europe.

July: *Gang Signs & Prayer* is nominated for a Mercury Award.

11 July: After teaming up with Ibiza Rocks to host a grime festival in Ibiza, #Merky Festival is held for the first time.

September: Presented with the GQ Solo Artist of the Year Award.

5 September: Wins Most Played New Independent Act and Album of the Year at the AIM Independent Music Awards, after also being nominated for Independent Track of the Year, with 'Big For Your Boots'.

October: Wins Best Solo Artist at the Q Awards, after also being nominated for Best Album with *Gang Signs & Prayer*.

24 October: Wins Artist of the Year and Best Video with 'Big For Your Boots' at the Rated Awards, after also being nominated for Best Track and Best Album.

27 October: Releases the single 'Blinded by Your Grace, Pt. 2'. The single hits #7 in the UK Singles Chart, #4 in the UK R&B Chart, and #1 in the UK Independent Chart, eventually going Platinum.

12 November: Wins Best Worldwide Act at the MTV EMAs, after also being nominated for Best UK & Ireland Act.

29 November: Wins three MOBO Awards - Best Grime, Best Male, and Best Album with *Gang Signs & Prayer* – after also being nominated for Best Video and Best Song with 'Big For Your Boots'.

5 December: Spotify announces its yearly statistics and reveals *Gang Signs & Prayer* was the fourth most-listened to album in the country, with over 123 million streams.

8 December: Wins Artist of the Year at the BBC Music Awards, with *Gang Signs & Prayer* also nominated for Album of the Year.

2018

January: Nominated for two NME Awards: Best British Solo Artist and Best Live Artist.

3 January: BBC report that Stormzy was the 9th most streamed artist of 2017.

19 January: Partners with Atlantic Records UK, making his label, #Merky, a joint venture.

21 February: Performs a freestyle at the Brit Awards in support of the victims of Grenfell, and also wins BRIT Awards for

British Male Solo Artist and British Album of the Year for *Gang Signs & Prayer*.

1 March: Wins two Global Awards, one for Best RnB, Hip Hop or Grime, and one for Best Song after lending vocals to Little Mix's song 'Power'.

31 May: Wins Best Album at the Ivor Novello awards with *Gang Signs & Prayer*, after also being nominated for Best Song.

2-3 July: Headlines the second of his #Merky Festivals in Ibiza.

7 July: Headlines Wireless Festival.

16 August: Announces The Stormzy Scholarship in partnership with the University of Cambridge.

2019

25 April: 'Vossi Bop' is released and debuts at #1 in the UK Singles Chart.

discography

Stormzy lyrics published by kind permission of
Warner/Chappell Music Limited

Studio Albums

Gang Signs & Prayer
Released: 24 February 2017
Label: #Merky Records
Format: CD, digital download
Producer: Stormzy, Fraser T Smith, 169, E.Y Beats,
    Mura Masa, Sir Spyro, SOS, Sunny Kale, Swifta Beater,
    Wizzy Wow, XTC
Chart Position: No. 1 UK Albums Chart
Singles: 'Big For Your Boots', 'Cold', 'Cigarettes & Cush',
    'Blinded by Your Grace, Pt. 2'

Extended Plays

Not That Deep (with The HeavyTrackerz)
Released: 20 June 2014
Label: TRKRZ Records
Format: digital download
Producer: The HeavyTrackerz

Dreamer's Disease
Released: 20 July 2014
Label: Self-released

Format: digital download
Producer: 1st Born, Foozine, The HeavyTrackerz, JRocs,
    TobiShyBoy

Mixtapes

168: The Mixtape
Released: 20 March 2013
Label: Self-released
Format: digital download
Producers: Dice Beats, Hopsin, Phantastik, Wisper

Other Singles

'Know Me From'
Released: 8 March 2015
Label: Self-released
Format: digital download
Producer: Zdot

'Wicked Skengman 4'
Released: 10 September 2015
Label: Self-released
Format: digital download
Producer: Stormzy

'Scary'
Released: 2 September 2016
Label: Self-released
Format: digital download
Producer: Sir Spyro

'Vossi Bop'
Released: 25 April 2019
Label: #Merky/Atlantic
Format: digital download/streaming
Producer: Chris Andoh

list of illustrations

All photographs in the book have been used courtesy of
Kaylum Dennis, unless stated otherwise below.

Section 1:

'Flipz said remember the talks that we had on the road, and
    never lose sight of the dream' [top and bottom]: © Stormzy
Kaylum: © Mabdulle (www.mabdulle.com)
'Wicked Skengman 2' video, February 2014: © Jaiden Ramgeet
'Went Jools Holland in my tracksuit, rep for the scene like
    yeah man I had to': © Stormzy
'We've got ten man chasing a dream': © Jaiden Ramgeet
Akua: © Filmawi Efrem (www.filmawi.com)

Section 2:

Tour life, Europe and America [bottom]: © Jaiden Ramgeet
First MOBO: ©Tristan Fewings/Getty Images
Ghana trip with Twin B: © Stormzy
'Know Me From' video, February 2015: © Jaiden Ramgeet
The Brit Awards and Red Bull Culture Clash, 2015 [top]:
    © Gareth Cattermole/Getty Images
The Brit Awards and Red Bull Culture Clash, 2015 [bottom]:
    © Jim Dyson/Getty Images for Red Bull
'Shut Up' video, May 2015: © Jaiden Ramgeet

AJ: © Stormzy

BBC 1Xtra Live, Leeds: © Andrew Benge/Redferns

'I might sing but I ain't sold out': © Ollie Millington/Redferns

Rachel: © Rachel Campbell

'Man just talk, don't talk, be steady': © Jaiden Ramgeet

Europe, London, V Festival, 2016 [top and bottom left]: © Stormzy

[Page 8, top]: © Andrew Benge/Redferns

[Page 8, bottom]: © Samir Hussein/Redferns

Section 3:

Studio life, part 1 [top right and bottom]: © Stormzy

'Team #Merky on the campaign trail': © Mabdulle
   (www.mabdulle.com)

[page 5, top and bottom]: © Mabdulle (www.mabdulle.com)

[Page 6, top]: © Charles McQuillan/Getty Images for Stormzy

Glastonbury, 2017 [top]: © Timms/Backgrid

'I stay prayed up then I get the job done': © Stormzy

[page 7]: © Mabdulle (www.mabdulle.com)

Section 4:

All images in this section are copyright © Kaylum Dennis, unless stated otherwise below.

'Wireless 2018': © Mabdulle (www.mabdulle.com)

The publisher and author have made every effort to credit the copyright owners of any material that appears within, and will correct any omissions in subsequent editions if notified.